Marvelous Minilessons

for Teaching Intermediate Writing Grades 3-8

Lori Jamison Rog

Pembroke Publishers Limited

© 2018 Lori Jamison Rog

Pembroke Publishers
538 Hood Road
Markham, Ontario, Canada L3R 3K9
www.pembrokepublishers.com

Distributed in the U.S. by Stenhouse Publishers
www.stenhouse.com

Library and Archives Canada Cataloguing in Publication

Rog, Lori Jamison, author
    Marvelous minilessons for teaching intermediate writing, grades 3–8 / Lori Jamison
Rog.

Issued in print and electronic formats.
Marvelous minilessons for teaching intermediate writing, grades 3–8.
ISBN 978-1-55138-329-3 (softcover).—ISBN 978-1-55138-930-1 (PDF)

    1. English language--Composition and exercises--Study and teaching (Elementary).
2. Report writing--Study and teaching (Elementary). 3. Language arts (Elementary).
I. Title.

LB1576.R66 2018   372.62'3   C2017-908005-9
                                       C2017-908006-7

Editor: Alyssa Rowley, Alison Parker
Cover Design: John Zehethofer
Typesetting: Jay Tee Graphics Ltd.

Printed and bound in Canada
9 8 7 6 5 4 3 2 1

FSC
www.fsc.org
MIX
Paper from
responsible sources
FSC® C004071

Contents

Chapter 8: Conventions: The Good Manners of Writing 119

Introduction: The "Writingest" Generation

Welcome to the "writingest" generation in history! Where writing was once the domain of the few and reading the domain of the many, today everyone is a writer. Your students are more likely to interact with their friends by text message than by phone or even in person. They blog, tweet, follow, friend, chat, and poke. There's no longer any special knowledge or expertise required to post a restaurant or hotel or business review; anyone with a smartphone is an expert.

According to the National Council of Teachers of English (NCTE) document "Writing in the 21st Century" (Yancey, 2009), "This 21st century writing marks the beginning of a new era in literacy, a period we might call the Age of Composition, a period when composers become composers not through direct and formal instruction alone, but through what we might call an extracurricular social co-apprenticeship" (p. 5).

For today's young people, literacy is no longer just a private world of a reader and a book; it is a social world of texting, blogging, and tweeting. And along with it, a whole new set of conventions that can set a literacy teacher's teeth on edge. The challenge for us as teachers is to meet our students where they are and honor what they know and can do, while helping them understand when emojis and SMS abbreviations are acceptable and when conventional grammar and spelling are *de rigeur.*

But grammar and spelling are not enough. In his work on 21st century skills, Tony Wagner (2008) identified written communication as one of the seven essential skills for success. According to Wagner, concerns about writing are not so much about the conventions of English as they are about fuzzy thinking and lack of voice. There is hardly a profession today that does not require workers to document ideas or write reports. A vice-president of a large telecommunications company recently told me that he has to rewrite almost everything his young employees submit to him. Spelling and mechanics are not the problem, he says. But they use too many words to say simple things and often, in an effort to use impressive vocabulary, even misuse those words. In all walks of professional life, writers must learn to be clear and concise, focused and energetic. And that's something computers can't do for us.

Writing is more important than ever in order to succeed in school. Writing is a tool that helps learners organize ideas, solve problems, and distinguish the important from the merely interesting. It allows students to reflect on different perspectives, and enables us to communicate our ideas to others as well as to document our thinking for ourselves. In the renowned 90/90/90 schools study, Douglas Reeves (2005) analyzed schools with 90% of students living in poverty, 90% belonging to ethnic minorities, and 90% testing at or above grade level in reading. What enabled these schools to beat the odds? Among other common factors, all of these schools focused on writing every day, in every subject. Writing was found to help students organize and clarify their thinking and provided teachers with richer diagnostic information than simply right or wrong answers on tests. In addition, the most successful schools used professional time to collaborate on both planning and assessment. When teachers sat down to score student writing together, they benefitted from more consistent grading practices as well as a common language and common understanding of the qualities of good writing.

This is not radical thinking. Over 100 years ago, the National Educational Association's "Committee of Ten on Secondary School Studies" (1894) wrote: "The study of every other subject should contribute to the pupil's training in English; and the pupil's capacity to write English should be made available and be developed in every other department." When the 90/90/90 schools focused on literacy and numeracy, the students progressed in other subject areas as well. As Reeves (2005) notes, "It is difficult to escape the conclusion that an emphasis on writing improvement has a significant impact on student test scores in other disciplines" (p. 190).

But if our students are going to use *writing to learn* effectively, they must have opportunities for *learning to write*. It's not enough to "do writing" as part of Science or Health or Mathematics or Reading. There must be a regular and frequent slot in the timetable dedicated to making students better writers. "Writing is a critical skill, important in its own right; given the evidence that consistent writing time and instruction not only improves writing but also reading, gives us an even more compelling case for finding time in our school day for more writing" (Tracy, 2013 n.p.).

Today, the majority of students in our schools have access to computers for learning. Word processing software enables writers to write longer pieces, make revisions and edits more easily, and produce completed work that looks practically professional. The *Writing Next* Report (Graham & Perin, 2007), found that word processing was one of the instructional innovations that has had a significant impact on the quality of student writing, especially for low-achieving students. Students who word process their writing tend to write longer pieces and are more willing to revisit and revise them.

However, in spite of the availability and efficacy of word processors, at the time of this writing, most students in Grades 3–8 are doing most of their writing by hand, even if they might word-process their "published" copy. This is not necessarily a bad thing. Weak keyboarding skills can interfere with the flow of composition. Spellcheckers absolve students of the responsibility to spell words correctly—and they often "miscorrect," substituting the wrong homophone, for example. Finally, there is compelling new research about the value of handwriting to document thinking (Waterman et al., 2017).

The Writing Workshop is a structure for teaching students the strategies that writers use, then giving them opportunities to practice and apply those strategies. As the term "workshop" implies, this is a place for experimenting and making messes, fixing those messes and starting over, cheering successes and celebrating accomplishments. It is a structure that supports self-regulation and independence, requiring writers to make their own decisions about what to write, what to publish, and how to make use of their writing time. Most importantly, it meets every writer where she is, and nudges each one to higher levels of proficiency. That's why our struggling writers often respond well to the Writing Workshop structure—because it's geared to their success and growth, not to their weaknesses.

The Minilesson

If the heart of the Writing Workshop is student writing, its head might be the minilesson. Usually—but not necessarily—at the start of the workshop, the minilesson is an opportunity to provide brief and explicit teaching in an aspect of the writing process or a writing strategy. How to craft an effective conclusion, how to prune your writing to eliminate unnecessary details, how to decide whether or not to use an apostrophe: all of these are examples of writing minilessons.

For many teachers, the biggest challenge is not *what* to teach, but *how* to teach writing. The great thing about writing instruction is its simplicity. No special resources are needed, other than something to write on and something to write with. We show students what writers do by modeling writing ourselves. As we write, we are constantly thinking aloud about the decisions we make as we choose our words or reflect on how to put those words together. Interestingly, our shortest lessons may very well be our most effective. That's the philosophy behind the *minilesson*—a brief and intentional instructional routine that focuses on a specific learning goal or writing strategy. Here are features of effective minilessons:

- **One specific learning goal:** Target a writing strategy that focuses on what we want our writers to know or be able to do. Make sure it's a strategy that students can transfer to other writing situations. Focus on only one goal at a time. A combination of your local curriculum standards/outcomes and your own ongoing assessments of your students will provide you with more lesson ideas than you'll ever have time to use.
- **A catchy name for the strategy that students will be able to hang on to:** Make sure students know what it is they're learning, in language they'll be able to understand and apply. Students will remember "Bossy Sentences" better than imperatives or commands.
- **Brevity:** Remember that it's a minilesson, not a maxilesson! Most of the workshop time should be dedicated to writing, not teaching. Sometimes it might be helpful to time the lesson and stop after 10 or 15 minutes. You can always continue the next day.
- **Modeling:** The very best way to teach children what writers do is to show them. Model writing for the students, "thinking aloud" your own process of getting the words on the page (or screen). Sometimes you'll compose the text yourself, sometimes you'll use an example from published literature, and sometimes you'll invite the students to collaborate in composing the text while you scribe, showing them what their words look like in print.
- **Guided practice:** Give the students a chance to try out the strategy in a safe and supportive setting, whether as a large group "shared writing" experience, in pairs, or in small groups.

- **Accountability:** Establish the expectation that students should use what they learned in the minilesson. If we've taught a lesson on powerful leads, for example, students should work on leads in their own writing.
- **Repetition:** Don't expect that all your students will master a concept or strategy after one 10-minute minilesson. Repeating a lesson several times—in large or small targeted groups—will help ensure that your students can master the habits of highly effective writers.

Of course, the minilesson is only a small part of the Writing Workshop. It's the "I DO" of the Gradual Release of Responsibility. The bulk of the Writing Workshop must be dedicated to guided practice ("WE DO"), and independent application ("YOU DO").

That's what the lessons in this book are about. Our students can't effectively write to learn if we don't give them opportunities to learn to write. They need to be able to articulate their thinking with clarity and voice, to use the most powerful words and craft them in the most effective ways. And we need to teach them.

How to Use This Book

Readers of the previous edition of this book, *Marvelous Minilessons for Teaching Intermediate Writing, Grades 4–6*, will recognize many of the lessons. But here are some features that make this book unique:

- The book is divided into three parts. The first focuses on organizing and managing the writing program, with tips on Writing Workshops and unit planning. The second section contains complete units on Writing to Learn, Writing to Inform, and Writing to Persuade, along with minilessons and assessment rubrics. The third part of the book comprises a collection of minilessons in three main areas of writing: Content (topics, details, and organization); Craft (word choice, voice, and fluency); and Conventions (spelling and mechanics).
- Each minilesson begins with a specific learning goal and is structured around teacher modeling and instruction (I DO), some guided practice in large or small groups (WE DO), and an expectation of independent application (YOU DO).
- The guided practice components of the lessons usually take the form of shared or interactive writing. In shared writing, the students collaboratively compose the text, while the teacher scribes. In interactive writing, the group composes the text together, but students take turns doing the writing.
- Some lessons may take more time than others. Be sensitive to the needs and interests of your students, but be careful not to take away too much time from student writing. Feel free to end midway through a lesson or continue it another day.
- Some lessons will include a literature link from a novel or picture book, but we should never use writing time for the first reading of any text. Read any book first as readers, and then revisit it as writers to analyze the techniques the writer has used.

This book is intended to offer a buffet of minilesson ideas to use as part of a balanced diet of writing instruction. Not every minilesson will be appropriate for every class, or even every student within a class. You are encouraged to pick and choose the lessons that meet your objectives for individuals and small groups. These lessons are not intended to be a complete year's curriculum, but rather a bank of ideas to add to your teaching repertoire.

Most importantly, I encourage you to *adapt* rather than *adopt* these minilessons. Make them your own and use language and models that work for you. Gather your own writing samples and literature links that you'll be able to use to reinforce the writing strategies you are teaching.

In any classroom, your students will be at many different places in their writing development. Only by careful observation and assessment of our students' writing can we provide the "just in time" instruction that will scaffold our students from where they are right now to where they have the potential to be.

Not every student of writing will become a published author, just as not every pianist will perform at Carnegie Hall, and not every junior hockey player will win the Stanley Cup. But, that doesn't mean we should give up on them. Instead we should encourage all writers to be the best they can be. In education, our job is not to create superstars, but to help the everyday stars in our classrooms to shine a little brighter.

Chapter 1

Writing Workshop: A Predictable Structure Where the Unpredictable Can Happen

> "You are never finished writing until writing time is up."
> — The "Golden Rule" of Writing Workshop

Does the mere mention of a "Writing Workshop" conjure up images of mountains of marking and classroom chaos? If the idea of every student working on different projects at different stages and at different times makes your head spin, then please read on! The Writing Workshop is anything but a free-for-all; it's a highly predictable structure (where the unpredictable can happen, according to researcher Lucy Calkins). Not only that, the Writing Workshop might very well be the best classroom routine we have for building student independence and self-regulation. After all, school shouldn't be a place where adults do the work for kids!

The very term "workshop" implies an opportunity to create and experiment and mess up and try again. The bonus of the Writing Workshop is that it meets every writer where she is. For some of your students, this might be the only time in the day when the work isn't too hard for them. Many struggling learners respond well to this structure in which they are empowered to make their own decisions about what to write, what to revise, what to publish, and what to abandon. They also learn to manage their own time. The "Golden Rule" of Writing Workshop is: "You are never finished writing until the time is up." (And what a gift for teachers never to hear, "What do I do when I'm done?") It is an expectation that students will use all of the writing time for writing; it's a further expectation that they will decide how to make good use of their time. If they finish one task, they move on to another.

> Choice, Time, and Response are the hallmarks of the Writing Workshop.

Of course, this means that students will be working on different projects and different stages of the writing process at the same time. Because they are expected to try out any strategies that are taught in the workshop, there will be times that all the students might be working on the same or similar tasks, but then they will work on projects of their own choice. It's unrealistic to expect writers at any stage to prewrite, draft, revise, edit, and publish on schedule. Anyone who writes knows that some pieces take a long time to plan and the rest goes very quickly, while other pieces start off with a bang but take ages to revise and get right. Every piece is different and every writer is different. There's also a big advantage for teachers in having students functioning independently at different stages of writing: we don't have to conference and prepare for publication with every student at the same time.

Choice is one of the hallmarks of the Writing Workshop. Time and response are the others. Writers need regular and consistent time for writing. And they need frequent feedback from other writers—peers and teachers—to improve their craft.

The Writing Workshop can take somewhat different forms in different classrooms with different teachers and students. The basics are: a little bit of explicit teaching, a big chunk of student writing time, and a reflection and sharing period at the end. It sounds simple. But fitting in all these pieces requires a 45 to 60-minute period. The teaching time is brief—only about 10–15 minutes for some explicit instruction and guided practice. The largest component is writing time—at least 25–30 minutes so students have time to dig deeply into their writing. Some students might finish a piece or take a break from a particular piece of writing at that time. Then they have to decide what to work on next. Taking responsibility for making good use of writing time is an important part of self-regulation. The final 10 minutes or so of Writing Workshop is a time to share and celebrate each other's writing. We've traditionally called this routine the "author's chair," though in intermediate classrooms, we're more likely to use a podium (or music stand) than a chair.

THE WRITING BLOCK
Teaching Time: 10–15 minutes
Writing Time: 25–30 minutes
Sharing Time: 10–15 minutes

How Can We Find the Time?

So how do we find up to an hour every day—or several times a week—for a writing block? Well, we might start by stealing some time from the reading block. We all know that reading makes kids better writers. But did you also know that writing makes kids better readers? In their treatise on *Writing to Read*, Steve Graham and Michael Hebert (2010) offer compelling evidence that teaching students about the process of writing, constructing sentences and paragraphs, and logically framing and communicating ideas actually improves reading comprehension.

"The evidence is clear: writing can be a vehicle for improving reading" (Graham and Hebert 2010, p. 6).

Dividing the Literacy Block between reading and writing (with word study woven freely between them) ultimately benefits both. Maybe we can justify spending three days a week on the reading block and two days a week on the writing block, say, Monday–Wednesday–Friday for reading and Tuesday–Thursday for writing?

Here's another way to find time for writing that might just shock you: scrap the grammar lessons! There's almost a century of research finding that traditional grammar instruction has, at best, *no impact* on improving writing—and some studies that show it can even be detrimental (Graham & Perin, 2007). If we want our students to use verb tenses, punctuation. and other grammatical constructs correctly, then we need to teach those lessons in situations where there is immediate application; in other words, the Writing Workshop. (You'll find a collection of minilessons and tips for instruction in the conventions of writing in Chapter 8).

And finally, a third option for grabbing time for writing: implement a Writing Workshop instead of journals. Although dialogue journals have a long tradition in our literacy programs, we're finding they don't contribute that much to improving writing. Why not? No instruction and no accountability. As Graham and Perin (2007) found, without explicit teaching of the strategies writers use, as well as an expectation for young writers to apply those strategies, there is no improvement in overall writing proficiency.

So, now that we've found space in our timetable for 45–60 minutes of writing, at least three times a week, what are we going to do with that time?

Teaching Time, Writing Time, Sharing Time

The Writing Workshop is a very structured routine, and it's important that we teach, practice, reinforce, and set expectations for student behavior. Too often we've assumed that our students will simply learn to write by writing. So we've fallen into the trap of *assigning* rather than teaching. We tell students to "write a story" or "write a report." But what does this teach them about being better writers? Instead of focusing on the product—the story, the poem, the report—we need to pay attention to the strategies that writers use.

The gradual release of responsibility applies as much to writing instruction as to any other aspect of teaching and learning. That's why the writing block has three components: some explicit teaching ("I DO"), some guided practice ("WE DO"), and a large chunk of time for independent application ("YOU DO").

Teaching time shouldn't take away from valuable writing time! You might even want to set a timer to keep your instruction and guided practice on target. You can always continue the lesson the next day.

Although **Teaching Time** can take place any time during the Writing Workshop, most teachers like to open workshop time with a quick shot of explicit teaching and guided practice. This instruction usually takes the form of teacher modeling and thinking aloud, but might also include a literature link or student writing sample. The challenge for teachers is to keep this teaching *brief* and *focused*. That's why we call it a *mini*lesson. The lesson should be long enough to address a learning goal, but short enough to hold the students' attention.

At the beginning of the school year, many of our minilessons focus on workshop routines and procedures, such as what to do when you're "done," how to organize your writing folder, and prescriptions for the pain of revision. But as the year progresses, we spend more and more time teaching strategies, the tools writers use to convey a message. An extensive body of research confirms that teaching writing *strategies* is the most effective way to improve student writing (Graham et al., 2012). Strategies for intermediate writers range from crafting clever beginnings to combining words in rhythmical ways to revising ideas for clarity and effectiveness.

The "WE DO" part of the lesson enables the students to practice the focus strategy in a supported or guided setting. This collaborative writing experience might take the form of shared writing, in which the students help to compose the text while the teacher scribes, or interactive writing, in which the students take turns doing the scribing as well as generating the ideas. Often it will consist of a short guided writing task, in which the students work with partners to try out the strategy together.

Writing Time is the longest and most important part of the Writing Workshop. It takes most intermediate students at least 30 minutes or more to really dig into a piece of writing or to get two or three shorter tasks completed. Remember that most students are unlikely to be writing steadily for the whole time. In addition to drafting or revising a piece of writing, they might be researching a new topic, conferring with a partner, or word-processing a polished piece. For some classes, it might be necessary to gradually build the stamina for 30 minutes of writing, but before long, your students are likely to complain that they've run out of time, not out of tasks.

Here's where opportunity and accountability meet. Since students are expected to apply what they've learned in the minilesson, that will be the first thing they do during writing time. They might be asked to experiment with a creative ending or revise a piece by substituting more powerful verbs. (In this book, you'll find guided practice exercises for each of the minilessons.) When they've completed that task, they are free to work on projects of their own choosing. Some might be creating a plan or working on a rough draft. Others might be revisiting a piece to add details or change words. Still others might be conferring with a partner or teacher for feedback and advice.

In Writing Workshop, students are responsible for using their time responsibly. That means that when they finish one task, they move on to another—independently and without teacher intervention. The first and most important routine in Writing Workshop is what to do when you're "done." There are basically three choices: finish a piece you started on a previous day; make some changes or revisions to a rough draft or work in progress; or start a whole new piece of writing. Of course, other activities such as teacher or peer conferences will also take up part of Writing Time, but these three activities—start a piece, finish a piece, revise a piece—are the foundation. The Writing Log (page 22) is a terrific tool for organizing and planning, but, of course, completing it should be modeled and practiced, just like any other lesson.

For most of us, writing is a social activity. We share our thinking, read bits of our writing aloud, ask questions, seek advice, or simply talk as we work. This opportunity for social interaction is an important part of Writing Workshop and we need to teach students how to respectfully respond to each other's writing. But some writers find concentration difficult in the midst of a buzz of conversation and movement. That's why I like to start writing time with 10 minutes of silence, dubbed "The Quiet Ten" by author Jennifer Jacobson (2010). I usually play soft music during this time; when the music stops, the students can move about and talk with others, but the Quiet Ten involves silent, individual writing time. For students who still need a little more solitude, cardboard carrels can be used as "private offices" to separate them from the classroom milieu.

As Writing Time draws to an end, it's beneficial to take time for sharing and reflection. Because we have just 5–10 minutes for Sharing Time, only two or three students can share their writing each day. It is both a privilege and a responsibility to share one's writing and every student will take a turn. I designate two students each day. Running down the class list, I announce at the beginning of Writing Workshop the names of the two students who will share at the end of that day's workshop. During Writing Time, these designated students must select a piece of writing and practice reading it aloud. They may read any piece—published or draft—as long as they haven't read it to the class before in the same form. (A piece may be reread if it has been revised in some way.) For some students, it might be necessary for the teacher to help them practice reading their writing aloud and, in exceptional cases, the teacher might read the piece for them. However, reading the piece aloud ensures that the listeners will focus on the content and style, and no one will know how well or how poorly the words are spelled or the sentences punctuated.

We treat these student writers just as we would a professional writer. We start by giving them "stars"—what we like about their writing or what they've done well. Then we ask questions or "wishes"—aspects of the writing that we don't understand or wish we knew more about. At first, students might struggle to find the language they need in order to offer constructive feedback to another writer. It's common to hear students say, "I liked it" or "It was funny." We need to prompt students to explain these comments further to help students identify *what* they liked, *what* was funny, or *what* the writer did well. And this is a great opportunity to model the kind of language students need to talk about writing—their own and that of others.

Early in the school year, it might be a little intimidating for some students to share their writing publicly. Of course, it's important to build an atmosphere of trust in the classroom for all intents and purposes. But even the most insecure writer soon learns that this is a time when everyone's writing is celebrated, not criticized. And there are few things more respectful to any writer than to hear, "I'm so interested in what you've written that I'd like to know more about it."

Supporting Independence

Empowering youngsters to make choices about their learning not only increases motivation, it reduces behavior problems, supports quality and effort for the task at hand and even promotes the general wellbeing of the learner (Kohn, 1993).

There are several ways in which Writing Workshop supports independent learning. We've already discussed the "Golden Rule" of Writing Workshop: "You're never done writing." When students are expected to "finish a piece, revise a piece, or start a new piece," they are learning to manage their own time.

The Writing Log (page 22) might very well be the most useful tool in the Writing Workshop. Students use the first few minutes of Writing Time to record the date and what they plan to work on. Usually the first task will be come from the minilesson, such as, "Find a place to insert slo-mo writing into my personal narrative" or "Revise fuzzy facts in my research piece." Because this task is unlikely to occupy the whole Writing Time, the writer should also plan what he is going to do next, such as "Start research on Pluto" or "Edit my persuasive piece." Planning is an important part of Writing Time. As soon as they record their plans, students should leave their Writing Logs out for the teacher to see and then get right to their writing.

As students complete their Logs, the teacher circulates around the room for a quick perusal. If a student's plan looks satisfactory, don't interrupt him! Just let him keep on writing and move on to the next student. Use this time to check on plans that seem inadequate or unclear and to help students who can't seem to get started.

When students are comfortable with recording their plans each day, you might want to add a reflection component to the Writing Log. Allow a couple of minutes at the end of Writing Time for students to record what they actually accomplished. (On the other hand, you may decide not to have them complete a written reflection; instead, as students gather for Sharing Time, give them a minute or two to tell a partner how they used their Writing Time.)

Of course, explicitly teaching students how to complete their Writing Logs is an essential minilesson in the early days of the Writing Workshop and it may take several days of modeling and guided practice before students are able to plan their time effectively. Start by displaying a blank Writing Log and think aloud as you write your plans for the day. Then have students talk to a partner before completing their own Writing Logs.

The Writing Log is not only a useful planning tool for students, it is a valuable assessment mechanism for teachers, especially when you can compare each student's plans and reflections. The Writing Log can offer a snapshot of how well students use their Writing Time and what stages of the writing process they are accomplishing.

Topic Self-Selection

With the exception of occasional guided writing tasks that are assigned to practice a strategy, our students are expected to choose what they're going to write about and what form it will take. At first, this is challenging for some students, especially those who haven't had a rich range of life experiences, or those who haven't had opportunities to make such choices in the past.

All writers are more engaged when they write about topics that matter to them. They write more and they write better. Research has shown that when students are interested in a topic, they pay more attention, sustain that attention for longer periods of time, and acquire more knowledge than they do with topics of less interest (Hidi & Anderson, 2014).

I often hear teachers say: "But my students don't have anything to write about!" Students need to see that anything can be an interesting topic, depending on how the writer treats that topic. (Poet Shel Silverstein has written poems about everything from hiccups to boxes—and even a toilet plunger.) It's important that we model writing about everyday topics and show students how to use rich details to make topics interesting to readers. Consider using shared school experiences such as a recent school assembly, an interesting class read-aloud, a playground dispute or a topic of study. (See page 84, The "Big Ideas" Bag.)

The truth is, the more a person writes, the easier it is to think of something to write about. People who write for a living will tell you that they have more ideas in their heads than they'll ever have an opportunity to use. On the other hand, the last thing we want is for students to waste valuable Writing Time pondering a topic. You can find lessons and ideas for topic selection throughout this book.

Managing Materials

One of the many great things about Writing Workshop is that you don't need any special materials—just something to write on and something to write with. Although the majority of intermediate students have access to computers and other word processing tools, many of them still compose with pen and paper and use the computer only for publishing. However, whether they draft with pen or with processor, it's important to make their revisions visible. That's why we use pens instead of pencils: to avoid erasing. And why we ensure that students date, save, and/or print a copy of their word-processed writing at the end of each Writing Workshop.

Sometimes, paper management can be a challenge. There are many workable systems for writing portfolios, but what works for me is a three-pocket folder. The three pockets are labeled: **Writing Ideas** (to store planning or brainstorming sheets or a Writer's Notebook); **Works in Progress** (drafts that are incomplete); and **Finished Drafts**.

To make a writing folder, simply find a large sheet of tagboard or Bristol board. Fold up the bottom third to form a pocket. Fold the entire folder into three vertical folds. Use a long-armed stapler to separate the three pockets. Label the pockets and have students decorate their own covers and laminate them, if they wish. Now your folders are ready to go—and they store easily in storage cubes readily available from your nearest big box store.

Even a writing folder can become unwieldy if it contains too many pieces of paper. That's why students store only three writing pieces at a time. My rule of thumb is: Draft three, publish one. For every three pieces they write, students

select one piece to revise, edit, and take to publication. The flip side of this rule is that students must write three drafts for every published piece. Note that the students themselves choose which pieces they're going to publish. These are the pieces on which we'll have formal (TAG) conferences (see page 18) and on which students will do both revision and editing. At the end of this cycle, the students submit the published piece and all three drafts for grading. (Sometimes, for example, students will have tried out a strategy on a rough draft that didn't make it to publication. Also, rough drafts are the perfect place to evaluate "no-excuse" spelling—the high frequency words that must be spelled correctly in everything they write.)

Publishing, in educational parlance, is simply sharing writing with an audience. Not every piece merits publication, and the ones that do get special attention to make them as interesting, clear, and error-free as possible, as a courtesy to our readers. You can read more about The Publication Journey in Chapter 3.

The Handwriting Dilemma

Is cursive writing obsolete? Many of us abandoned handwriting instruction a few years ago because no one beyond the classroom ever seemed to use it. Every adult I know uses a computer or, if necessary, prints in block letters (other than the squiggle they call their signature). But there's increasing research on the benefits of writing information by hand rather than word processing (Waterman et al., 2014). Believe it or not, handwriting is good for your brain! Writing on paper stimulates neural pathways that keep your brain sharp and active. Plus, material written by hand is retained in memory much longer. So, don't put those pens away just yet!

The Teacher's Role

With all this student independence, what's left for the teacher to do? When we don't need to spend our time managing behavior, we can dedicate it to practices that make our students better readers, writers, and thinkers! Writing Time is a wonderful opportunity to offer just-in-time teaching in the form of individual writing conferences. I do three types of conferences: The Walkabout (otherwise known as the Bumblebee conference), the TAG conference for revision, and the final Polish to Publish, or editing, conference.

The Walkabout Conference

I've called these **Walkabout Conferences** many different names over the years, but the principle remains essentially the same: at the start of Writing Time, I "buzz" around the room like a bumblebee, alighting at every student's workspace to look at their Writing Logs and to make sure everyone is getting started. If I have a question for the student about her plans for the day, I'll stop and pose it, but I try to avoid interrupting a student who is already engaged in writing. At this point, I focus on students who have a problem to deal with or who seem unable to get started. Once everyone is off to a good start, I can dedicate my time to TAG Conferences.

The TAG Conference

TAG is an acronym for: **T**ell something you like; **A**sk questions; **G**ive advice.

The TAG Conference may very well be my favorite part of the Writing Workshop, because it gives me one-on-one time with students to target specific needs in their writing. The acronym TAG stands for Tell something you like, Ask questions, and Give advice. This is actually a *revision* conference in preparation for publishing, so the focus is on content, clarity, and craft; there will be an opportunity to look at spelling and conventions later. I always start by identifying strengths in the writing, *telling* the writer things he or she has done well. Then I will *ask* the writer some questions about the writing, either to clarify the content or to discuss decisions the writer has made. For example, I might say, "What happened when your cat jumped in the bathtub?" Or, "Why did you decide to end the piece in this way?" Finally, I will *give some advice*—suggestions to help make the writing more interesting, more coherent, or more eloquent.

Here's a tip when conferring with writers from Kindergarten to College: Never leave a conference without asking the writer to reiterate what revisions she is going to undertake.

For most student writing, I could offer plenty of suggestions; however, I'm going to limit myself to just a couple of things the writer will be able to apply to future writing. I don't want to put words in the writer's mouth; rather, I am going to make general suggestions that can apply to the writing, such as: "Why don't you add the detail about how your cat got out of the yard?" or, "We've talked about different ways to end a piece of writing. Please replace 'The End' with an ending that ties the bow on the present for a reader."

As a rule, we only have time for TAG conferences on pieces of writing that are going to be published. When a student has decided to take a piece to publication, she places it in my TAG Conference Basket. The student moves on to other writing until I am ready to call her up for the conference (usually a day or two later). This gives me time to review the piece and prepare my comments before the meeting.

If I'm going to give useful comments, I need to prepare ahead of time; I only have three or four minutes to spend with each student, so I need to make those minutes count. After the TAG conference, the student is expected to make the revisions we discussed. Although my recommendations are labeled "advice", they are not optional! The whole point of the exercise is to build strategies that will not only make each student's writing stronger, but that can be applied to other writing down the road.

> *Peer Conferences for meaning and clarity (page 100) can be a powerful experience for both writer and reader. However, I rarely have students edit each other's work for conventions. Often the peer editor doesn't know any more about the correct spelling and punctuation than the writer! And if they are already competent spellers, it's a waste of their own writing time to be correcting someone else's work.*

Five Tips For TAGs

1. Be specific. Comments like "good job" or "nice work" send writers a message that you didn't really pay attention.
2. Focus on ideas first—clarity, detail, effectiveness—then look at craft. This is not the time to talk about mechanics.
3. Make comments and suggestions that focus on the writing, not the writer. Comments like "You really know a lot about Space" aren't as useful as "You have a lot of interesting details about Space."
4. Asking for clarity or more information is a compliment to a writer! It says that you're interested enough to want to know more. Questions should focus on clarifying or elaborating on details in the piece.
5. Limit your advice to a couple of things. You're not going to turn a piece of Grade Five writing into a prize-winning novel. But you can help that writer learn something that will make him or her a better writer.

However brief, the TAG conference provides an opportunity to spend precious time with students and offer the just-in-time teaching that will nudge each student to higher levels of sophistication.

The Editing (Polish to Publish) Conference

The final step before taking a piece of writing to publication is the **Polish to Publish Conference** for repairing conventions. It's much easier for a reader to navigate a piece of writing when the writer has used conventional spelling and grammar. Our challenge as teachers is to decide what a writer needs to fix, what elements are teachable, and what can be left alone.

After a writer has completed the required revisions based on the TAG conference, that student is responsible for editing his own writing for conventions (see page 123). Don't expect miracles! It's very difficult for writers of any age to spot errors in their own work, but it's still an important process to teach students. When the writer has completed his own edits, he once again submits the writing, this time placing it into the Editing Basket, for a final teacher conference.

The teacher's task in this conference is to review the piece of writing to determine what that particular writer needs to fix. Choosing which errors to correct can be arbitrary and will vary for different writers and different situations. There are no hard and fast rules, except for identified "no-excuse words" that must always be spelled conventionally (see pages 121–122).

We look for spelling errors and grammatical structures that the writer should already know or are teachable in a short conference. Are there any patterns in the student's errors? Is there a guideline (such as *i before e)* that you might review or introduce? Be selective. Sitting with a student to correct error after error is not a good use of time for either of you. Reviewing a small number of errors leads to a better chance of a student's retention and application in future writing.

To Fix or Not to Fix?

Should the teacher act as the final copyeditor on all students' published writing—in other words, make all final corrections? I make that call based on how "public" the published piece will be. If it's going to be published for classroom use only, then I save my battles and only focus on a few "teachable" errors. I don't want my students to rely on me for their corrections.

However, if the writing is going out into the public, where the audience may not understand the process taught to young writers, I tend to fix many, if not all, the errors. In this way readers can focus on the message of the writing, not the number of spelling mistakes.

Writing Workshop and The Struggling Writer

Writing Workshop is an important structure for a number of reasons. It provides instruction and guided practice before expecting independent application. It builds independence and self-regulation. Most importantly, it meets every student where he or she is. Often our most vulnerable learners respond well to the Writing Workshop because this might be the only time in their day when work isn't too hard. Every student's work is celebrated in the Author's Chair, regardless of its sophistication. It is one of the few classroom routines in which every student can participate at her own level and progress at an individual pace to increasingly higher levels of achievement. In fact, there is evidence that students with learning disabilities respond particularly well to a process approach to writing, as long as they are taught the process and given opportunities to engage in meaningful writing tasks. (Marchisan and Alber, 2001).

Many of our students experience a crisis in confidence when it comes to writing. Writing is, after all, a public endeavor. When we write, our thoughts and ideas, even our feelings, are preserved for posterity—and so are our inadequacies. As a result, many students simply refuse to try. The opportunities for choice, the TAG Conference, and the Sharing Time are structures that help build both confidence and competence.

Struggling writers need the same good teaching as proficient writers—but they need it even more. Instruction that is guided by assessment and sensitive to student needs helps all learners. But struggling writers often need additional support such as:

• More opportunities for talk before, during, and after writing;

- Differentiated expectations, such as fewer drafts, additional teacher conferences, extra editing support and other detours on the Journey to Publication (page 25);
- Consistent routines and a predictable schedule;
- Less multitasking and more emphasis on one thing at a time, especially when it comes to revising and editing;
- More opportunities for word-processing;
- Explicit instruction in the use of resources such as dictionaries and thesauruses;
- Chunking of time and tasks, with breaks throughout the Writing Time;
- Gradual release of support and increase in independence.

Technology Talk

Many teachers have their students word-process their published writing. Word-processing makes the published piece look more professional and facilitates last minute revision and editing. But computers should be more than glorified typewriters in our intermediate writing classrooms. What can we do to provide a full range of writing experiences that take advantage of what technology has to offer, while balancing social networking communication and formal writing conventions?

1. **Familiarize students with keyboarding as early as possible.** This doesn't necessarily mean traditional "touch typing," but rather helping kids develop a system of automaticity with the keyboard. As long as students need to hunt and peck for every letter, simple typing will interfere with their thinking processes as they write. The whole point of keyboarding is to allow the writer's fingers to move as quickly as his or her brain. When keyboarding becomes automatic, students can plan and draft, as well as publish their writing on the computer.
2. **Require students to date and make a print copy of each draft.** It's too easy for intermediate students to mislay files, lose revisions, or fail to make changes at all. For instructional purposes, you need to see evidence of revision and proof of process, and, whether we like it or not, the hard copy is the most reliable.
3. **Teach the place for symbols and the place for standard spelling and mechanics.** There is no point in railing against emojis and abbreviations; instead, teach students when these typographic symbols are appropriate and when they're not.
4. **Encourage the publication of multimodal texts.** Not every type of writing requires a paper report with indented paragraphs and a title centered at the top. Encourage students to blend print and pictures, and teach them how to lay out a page efficiently, so a fancy design doesn't take precedence over well-crafted text.
5. **Combat the cut-and-paste culture generated by internet research.** Require students to use a variety of print and Web-based sources to gather information. Teach students how to be critical readers and to discern factual information from opinions and inconsistencies. Explain the difference between effective use of quotations, how to cite references, and the pitfalls of plagiarism. (See Chapter 4, "Writing to Inform," for ideas.)

Writing Log Template

Date	What I Plan to Work on Today	What I Got Done Today

Chapter 2   Where Do We Start?

Here's my favorite writing lesson for the first day of school. Fold a piece of paper in half. On one half, write the title "Love it!" and on the other half, write the title "Loathe it!" (Never miss an opportunity to teach a new vocabulary word!) Demonstrate for students as you list three or four things you absolutely *love* (foods, places, people, animals, things to do) and three or four things you absolutely *loathe* (anything but people). Then have the students do the same. Give them a few minutes to share their lists with a partner. This writing task is easy, guarantees success, and provides a ready-made list of topics for writing.

LOVE IT!	LOATHE IT!
· cinnamon buns	· olives
· Italy	· Daylight Savings time
· bike riding	· traffic
· singing	· cell phones in public places
· blue sky	· littering
· my babies	

Now demonstrate how you turn one of the topics on your list into a piece of writing. You might even give students an opportunity to choose one topic and tell their partners at least three details about that topic. (Allowing kids to talk before they write is especially important for struggling readers.) Invite them to choose a topic and just start writing—whatever they want about that topic. Here's your opportunity to introduce the "golden rule" of Writing Workshop: you're never done writing! Tell the students that if they finish the piece they're working on, they should choose another topic and start another piece. If they don't finish the piece, then they'll have time to work on it the next writing day.

The next day, continue writing about their "Love it or Loathe it" topics. Use your Teaching Time to demonstrate how you might go back into the previous day's piece of writing to add or change details. Then have students do the same thing. If you do this every day (or for several days), you'll have a little collection of short writing pieces from every student to assess for strengths and needs. Look for patterns of need: strings of details without elaboration; missing lead or conclusion; or run-on sentences? This assessment will guide you in planning future lessons.

At the same time, you might also be offering minilessons on classroom routines, such as how to complete a Writing Log, or finding a spot to write, or how to organize a writing folder. But this week of short self-selected writing pieces based on the "Love it or Loathe it" chart builds confidence and lets the students know right from the start that they will be writing every day, that they will be choosing what to write about, and that they will be deciding when a piece is finished or needs revision.

And what about the next week of school? And the week after that? It's quite possible to teach writing all year by selecting random lessons here and there from this book and other professional resources. I know—I've done it. But putting lessons together in units of study makes teaching easier, learning more coherent, and assessment more authentic. Effective unit planning enables teachers to present related content and skills in a seamless and sequential fashion over an extended period of time. And while frontloading planning might seem time-consuming (because it is), it's actually more time-efficient than planning lessons every day from scratch.

Planning Units of Study

We teachers plan all the time. We make lesson plans, daily plans, unit plans, and yearly plans. Usually we start with a special task, an engaging activity or a terrific lesson idea. However, there's considerable evidence to suggest that planning is a lot more effective when we start with what we want our students to know or to be able to do. That's why Grant Wiggins and Jay McTighe (1998) call this approach to curriculum planning "backward design"—because it's beginning with the end in mind. When we start with learning goals, we can plan the teaching that guides our students to reach those goals and create the assessment tools needed to measure our students' progress.

Traditionally, unit planning was subject-specific, based on a broad topic or concept related to a particular content area or cross-curricular theme, with reading and writing woven into the content. But writing frequently got shortchanged. All too often, writing became just a tool for learning rather than a learning goal in itself. If we want our students to be able to use writing effectively for learning and for communication, we need to build units of study around *learning to write* as well as *writing to learn*.

Teaching by Text Form

Some teachers prefer to teach by theme or topic; others like to build units around literary elements or writer's techniques. I prefer teaching by text form (a term which I'll use interchangeably with *genre,* even though purists would argue) because different text forms have unique structures, points of view, and even language features. Most importantly, different text forms perform different functions. When we want to convince someone to agree with our point of view, we use persuasive writing. When we want to tell a story, we use narrative writing. When we want to teach about or explain something, we use informational writing. When we want to show how to do something, we use procedural writing. And although the lines are sometimes blurred, or several formats combined in a single piece of writing, it's still useful for writers to know the most effective ways to use writing in order to serve their intended purposes.

It's generally agreed that intermediate students should know how to craft personal narrative, informational, and persuasive texts, as prescribed in the US Common Core State Standards. These three text forms could comprise the foundation of a year's writing curriculum, with one of these comprehensive units each term. (You can find complete units of study on informational and persuasive writing in Chapters 4 and 5 of this book.) The rest of the year could be spent on shorter units such as poetry, fictional narrative, and procedural writing, as well as many opportunities for self-selected writing.

The Journey to Publication

The other consideration in planning genre-based units of study is guiding students to take at least one piece of writing from conception to publication. Over the years, the term "writing process" has become ingrained in our pedagogical consciousness. We know that it is the natural way any writing is done. Think about writing a piece for the school newsletter or a report on a student. You consider what you're going to say, who's going to read it, and what form it's going to take; that's the *prewriting* phase. Then you *draft* your message, by hand or keyboard. And if you're the only one who's going to read that writing, there's nothing more that needs to be done with it. But if you're going to *publish* it, that is, share it with an audience beyond yourself, then you take time to review it for clarity and effectiveness (*revision*) and make sure all your T's are crossed and I's are dotted, metaphorically and literally speaking (*editing*).

This is actually quite a natural process, but it often needs to be made explicit for young writers. That's why any unit plan should include minilessons for planning, for turning that plan into a draft, and for revising and editing before publication. It should be noted that as adult writers, we often revise and edit at the same time. In fact, in professional parlance, it's all called "editing." But for novice writers, it's important to separate these two processes. Encourage them to make sure their message is clear, artfully articulated, and full of voice (*revision*) before expecting them to correct errors in spelling and conventions (*editing*). You'll notice that these are two separate conferences in the Writing Workshop (page 18).

We don't publish everything we write. As mentioned earlier, I expect students to draft three pieces for every one that they take to publication. When they have completed three pieces of writing, they select the one that they will revise and edit for publication. Revising is a hard sell for many young writers; in every other subject, when you need to go back in and change or fix something, it's because it is wrong or not good enough. But in writing, revising and editing are processes we do with our *best* work—to make it even better!

The "draft three, publish one" guideline for each unit is just that—a guideline. Some students will not complete three rough drafts (especially for units that require lengthy research) and some may go through the entire cycle more than once. As always, be sensitive to the strengths and needs of your students and differentiate as necessary.

Once a student has selected the piece of writing she wishes to publish, she puts it in the teacher's "TAG Conference" basket. This gives the teacher time to peruse the piece and plan for an effective and efficient conference. (See page 18

THE WRITING PROCESS
Planning/Prewriting – *Getting started*
Drafting – *Getting it down*
Revising – *Getting it good*
Editing – *Getting it right*
Publishing – *Getting it out*

Some teachers like to include a "peer conference" step prior to the teacher revision (TAG) conference. See page 100 for "Stars and Wishes" Peer Conferences.

for more information on the TAG conference.) Meanwhile, the student moves on with another piece of writing until the teacher can meet with her about the soon-to-be published piece.

After the TAG conference, the student goes back into the piece to make the suggested revisions. Now is the time to pay attention to spelling and conventions. Using a self-editing process such as the one described on page 123, the student makes any corrections she can, then places the piece in the teacher's "Editing Conference" basket. To prepare for the conference, the teacher reviews the piece and determines what surface edits the student should complete and which might be left alone. (See page 19 for more information on planning the editing conference.) After this conference, the student completes the required edits and is ready to publish her piece. This is often an opportunity to create a professional-looking word-processed piece, even if it has been drafted and revised by hand.

When a student has completed the journey to publication, I have him submit the three rough drafts and the published piece for evaluation. Sometimes the rough drafts can provide insights about the writer's process (not to mention his facility with spelling high-frequency words in all writing) and the final piece is evaluated according to the strategies that have been taught.

THE PUBLICATION JOURNEY

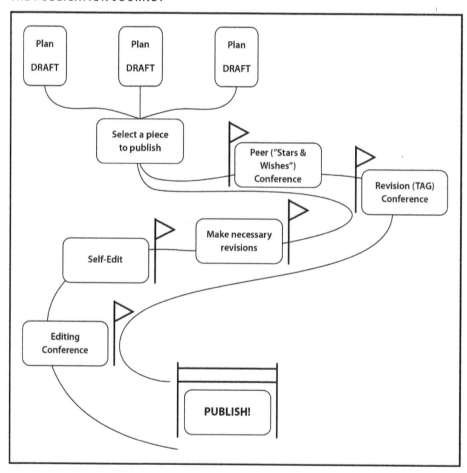

Planning a Genre-Based Unit of Study

Four Steps to Planning a Genre-Based Unit of Study in Writing

1. Outline the features of the text form.
2. Generate a set of learning goals for the students.
3. Plan a sequence of lessons to address each of the learning goals.
4. Assess student progress toward the learning goals.

1. Determine the features of the genre or text form that will be the focus of the unit. The elements of the text form will guide us in generating goals for learning to write that form.

SAMPLE QUESTIONS FOR CREATING A FRAMEWORK FOR A TEXT FORM

	Characteristics of the Text Form
CONTENT	• What kinds of topics and details are characteristic of this form? • How are the details organized? • Are there any unique text structures or formats?
WRITER'S CRAFT	• What purpose does this text form serve? • Is there a characteristic tone or mood ("voice")? Are there special techniques for creating that mood? • What kinds of vocabulary and literary techniques are common to this text form?
CONVENTIONS	• Which conventions are unique to this text form?

2. Determine a set of learning objectives for the unit. What do we want our students to know and be able to do as a result of this unit? The specific features of the text form—its unique organizational structure, perspective, and text features—guide us in generating learning goals for the students. Organizing the learning objectives around content (topics, details, and organization), craft (word choice, voice, and fluency) and conventions (punctuation and sentence structure) helps to balance instruction and provides students with the strategies they need to successfully navigate that text form.

The "Goldilocks principle" is the challenge here! How many objectives are not too many, not too few, but "just right"? It depends, of course, on a lot of things: the sophistication of your students, what they already know and can do, and the length of time you're prepared to spend on the unit. Remember that each learning goal must be taught and assessed, so you don't want to overwhelm yourself or your students. About ten learning objectives in a month-long unit would be manageable for teaching and learning—we're shooting for mastery here, not just dabbling in a bunch of strategies.

As you develop the learning goals, you'll want to consult your local curriculum for mandated objectives, aligned with your own classroom assessments of your students' needs.

www.ReadWriteThink.org is an excellent source of free literacy lesson ideas.

3. Plan a sequence of lessons to address each of the learning objectives. This is the easy part! It's not necessary to reinvent the wheel in order to create lesson plans. There are many resources available to help you teach the strategies your students need, including this book. The key is to focus on what students are learning as writers rather than on a cute or clever activity. Look for lessons that meet your specific learning goals. As you plan your lessons, consider the best order of presentation. Do some lessons serve as prerequisites for others? Is there a step-by-step component that should be considered? In Chapters 4 and 5 of this book, I show how this can be done with a sequence of minilessons that build on one another to go from planning to drafting to revising and publishing informational and persuasive writing.

Be sure to build in some flexibility in timing to accommodate unplanned "teachable moments." And, of course, be prepared to repeat lessons to achieve a particular objective; our students don't always "get it" the first time around!

Fortunately, the structure of the Writing Workshop lends itself to empowering each student to work at his or her own level, and consideration should always be given to accommodating individual differences.

4. Create an assessment plan and construct a rubric that is aligned with your learning goals. How will you know whether students have achieved the learning goals? Will you define degrees of mastery? Will you evaluate drafts and guided writing tasks as well as published work?

When I evaluate student progress for a report card grade, I think it's important to look at both product and process. The individual Writing Logs (page 22) are valuable sources of information about how the students have made use of their writing time. I often look at rough drafts for evidence of revision, editing or correct spelling of "no-excuse words" (pages 121–122). Sometimes, I will even give a writing "test" that asks students to revise an anonymous piece of writing or suggest "stars and wishes." And I always construct a rubric to guide me in measuring students' progress toward specific goals and to guide students in understanding the criteria for assessment.

> Some teachers invite students to hand in their final writing for a "freebie" assessment using the rubric. Then the students have the opportunity to go back and revise their writing before getting a final score.

Rubrics

A rubric is a rating scale that describes different levels of quality for different criteria. It is the best tool we have for assessing tasks where proficiency is difficult to quantify because there's no simple "right" or "wrong." Rubrics not only help teachers assign grades more easily and fairly, they clearly indicate the strengths and weaknesses of a piece of writing—and what the writer can do to improve it. That's why rubrics are useful for both formative and summative assessments.

You can find scores (pun intended!) of ready-made rubrics online and in print resources. But they're not particularly useful if they're not aligned with your specific learning goals. Ideally, we can work collaboratively with students to construct rubrics in language they understand. (But it's always a good idea to have a plan in mind before engaging the students in this process.) When they understand the criteria for quality writing, it helps both their initial drafts and subsequent revisions. When students understand what is expected of them, they are better able to strive to meet those expectations.

> Websites like rubistar.4teachers.org offer templates for creating different types of rubrics.

> *I often play "the scoring game" with intermediate students, in which we collaboratively assess anonymous pieces of writing and score them. Often, students will then be given the opportunity to revise those pieces of writing to try to raise the scores. It's amazing how much easier it is to revise someone else's writing! When students have an opportunity to work in collaborative groups to assess pieces of writing, they are more likely to internalize the knowledge and apply it to their own writing. When they are invited to work with others to revise a piece of writing by an anonymous writer, they are able to experiment without risk. They learn how to choose words that make writing more powerful, how to add detail to enhance a theme, and how to prune unnecessary information, building skills and strategies that, we hope, will transfer to their own compositions.*

If assessment is to be truly integrated with instruction, it must be continuous and ongoing—a starting point rather than an endpoint in the instructional process. Continual monitoring of student learning means that the lines between assessment and instruction fade to a perpetual cycle of assessing student progress toward educational goals and adapting instruction to help foster that progress.

Here are some simple guidelines for constructing rubrics:

1. *Determine how many levels your rubric will represent.* Rubrics commonly have four to six levels, although they can have as few as three or many more. When you use an even number, there's less tendency to lump scores in the middle.

2. *Select the criteria you want to assess.* Criteria on the rubric should be specifically aligned with the learning objectives in the unit. We don't assess anything we haven't taught.

3. *Determine what level is the "standard."* Some people feel that there is no need for more than one degree of inadequacy (i.e., one level below the standard), although others have made strong arguments in favor of showing students how close they are to achieving the standard.

4. *Create a description of each of the criteria at each level.* The best rubrics are descriptive enough to clearly distinguish each level from the next without leaving gaps. Try to use specific and descriptive language. General terms like *more* or *stronger* and subjective terms such as *creative* or *effective* may not be clear to either the evaluator or the one being evaluated. However, beware of limiting yourself by being too specific, such as "three details…" Are three mundane details superior to two excellent ones? Also, try to avoid combining two or more criteria into one description, as this creates a challenge when a writer has achieved one criterion but not another.

5. *Decide how the rubric will be used for grading.* Are all of the criteria weighted equally? Will you assign a score or a range of scores to each level? How will the rubric align with report card grades?

A Sample Unit Plan for Personal Narrative Writing

The following Unit of Study was developed by intermediate teachers who dedicated one of their summer professional development days to collaborative planning in writing. Together, we used the process just described to articulate learning objectives, plan lessons, and construct a rubric for the unit.

The teachers decided to start the year with personal narrative, or memoir writing, because it is a manageable text form for students and one of the writing forms mandated by their district. With memoirs, students don't need to imagine or research topics for writing and the general structure is already familiar to most of them from the primary grades.

The chart on page 31 encapsulates our unit plan, starting with characteristics of the text form in column 1, aligned learning goals in column two, and specific minilessons in column 3. For some teachers, starting with learning objectives rather than lesson activities represented a significant shift in their thinking. Others observed that the biggest challenge was to go "deep" rather than "wide;" in other words, to limit the number of learning goals to allow time for mastery. We ended up with ten learning objectives related to content (ideas and organization) craft (word choice, voice, fluency) and conventions (spelling and mechanics) to teach, practice, and apply in a 4–6 week unit, with Writing Workshop scheduled three times a week. There were many more objectives that we could have included, but we felt this was manageable for instruction and assessment. Our goal was to have each student write at least two, and possibly three, rough drafts and take one to publication during this time.

We chose to construct a five-level rubric, but decided to describe only Levels 5, 3, and 1, with the understanding that writing that surpassed one level but did not quite attain the next could be assigned a 2 or 4. (This also satisfies the universal teacher penchant for the "plus or minus.") We also felt that it was important to use language that students could understand, so that the rubrics could be used for self- and peer-assessment, as well as teacher conferences and evaluation. As well, we wanted the rubric to be flexible enough for teachers to adapt it to their needs, such as weighting some criteria more heavily than others.

The teachers found that collaborative planning like this was both instructional and time-efficient. They were able to provide students with a common language and instructional goals, while still allowing leeway for different teaching styles and diverse student needs.

You can find a complete sequence of lessons for the first six weeks of school based on this text form plan on page 32.

The Power of Collaborative Planning

When teachers plan together, they build common understandings and language—not to mention saving time and energy. Even when the grade levels are disparate, they can start with a common plan and adjust lessons and expectations according to grade levels and student needs.

TRAIT	CHARACTERISTICS OF THE TEXT FORM	LEARNING GOAL Students will be able to…	MINILESSONS * lesson is found in this book
CONTENT	– Tells the story of something that happened to the author (or someone else) – Details generally flow chronologically	– Choose details and elaboration to tell the about an experience that happened to them – Organize details in order with a beginning, middle and ending	Writing Ideas Bingo* Trifold Planner* From Plan to Draft Slo-Mo Writing*
CRAFT	– First person, storytelling voice – Contains plenty of descriptive vocabulary, including vivid verbs – Combinations of long and short sentences, varied sentence types, even fragments – Uses literary techniques such as similes and alliteration	– Speak to their reader and tell a story – Grab the reader's attention and wrap the piece up neatly – Energize their writing with vivid verbs – Use three different variety of sentence types to make writing flow.	TAP into Voice* Vivid Verbs* Dabble in Dialogue* Super Ways to Start Three Ways to End*
CONVENTIONS		– Capitalize and punctuate different types of sentences correctly – Use quotation marks for dialogue – Draft in paragraphs	Five Ps of Paragraphing* Sixty-Sixes and Ninety-Nines Edit Your Own Writing* Three Sentence Stories*

GETTING STARTED: THE FIRST SIX WEEKS

WEEK 1: *Gather short writing pieces for benchmark assessment and establish Writing Workshop Routines.*

- Love it or Loathe it
- Creating a writing folder
- Completing a Writing Log
- Drafting: Double-spaced and on one side of the paper
- Spell as well as you can

WEEK 2: *Introduce the Personal Narrative Text Form and begin planning.*

- What is a personal narrative? (Read a mentor text and discuss the characteristics of the text form.)
- Writing Ideas Bingo—Generating Topics
- The Trifold (Beginning, Middle, End) Planner

WEEK 3: *Continue modeling and practicing planners and introduce drafting.*

- Listing or Layering?
- TAP into Voice (From Plan to Draft)
- Five Ps of Paragraphing

WEEK 4: *Introduce writer's craft lessons to revise rough drafts.*

- Super Ways to Start
- Three Ways to End
- Slo-Mo Writing (Revise drafts to insert)
- Dabble in Dialogue (Revise drafts to insert or improve dialogue)
- Sixty-Sixes and Ninety-Nines (Quotation marks for dialogue)

WEEK 5: *Continue revising drafts and introduce peer conferences.*

- Vivid Verbs (revise drafts to replace mundane verbs)
- Three Sentence Stories (revise to insert questions and exclamations)
- Stars and Wishes Peer Conferences

WEEK 6: *Introduce editing for conventions and publishing.*

- Edit your own writing
- Polish to publish

	5	4	3	2	1
CONTENT	This writing is full of rich details and elaboration that tell an interesting story. Slo-Mo writing makes the most important part more exciting. This writing has a beginning that grabs the reader's attention, an interesting middle, and an ending that wraps the piece up neatly.		This writing stays on topic and has many interesting details. There seems to be some Slo-Mo writing. This writing has an interesting beginning, middle, and end. The details flow in an order that makes sense.		This writing seems to wander a bit. It might be missing important details. There is no Slo-Mo writing. This writing is sometimes hard to follow. Some of the details seem to be out of order. It might be missing a good opening or closing.
CRAFT	This writing is full of interesting words, especially vivid verbs. Some long and some short sentences, including questions and exclamations, make this writing sound good to the ear. Bits of dialogue (with correct punctuation) make the story more interesting. It's like the writer is telling a fascinating story right to the reader.		There are some interesting words in this piece, including a few vivid verbs. This writing contains at least one question and exclamation. Most of the sentences are about the same length. There is some dialogue in the story. This writing sounds "friendly" but pretty much all the same.		All the words in this piece are pretty ordinary. It's hard to tell where the sentences begin and end. Dialogue hasn't been used effectively (or correctly). This sounds like robot writing—a bit choppy and flat.
CONVENTIONS	All the words (except maybe a few hard words) are spelled correctly. Sentences have capitals and end punctuation.		Most of the ordinary words (except maybe a few hard ones) are spelled correctly. Most sentences have correct capitalization and end punctuation.		There are so many mistakes in spelling and sentence structure, that it's hard to read this piece of writing.

Chapter 3　Writing to Learn

> Q: Who was the villain in "Jack and the Beanstalk"?
> A: I think Jack was the real villain in "Jack and the Beanstalk". The giant was just minding his own business when Jack climbs up the beanstalk and steals his gold. There's no proof the giant ever ate a boy. The giant was only protecting his own property going after Jack. Who can blame him?

"If students are to learn, they must write" (Graham and Hebert, 2010).

Did you know that writing is the single best way to help you understand and remember what you read? It is even better than discussing or rereading, according to Steve Graham and Michael Hebert, in their meta-analysis of the research on writing to read. They concluded, "if students are to make knowledge their own, they must struggle with the details, wrestle with the facts, and rework raw information and dimly understood concepts into language they can communicate to someone else. **In short, if students are to learn, they must write"** (Graham and Hebert, 2010, p. 2).

In the renowned 90/90/90 schools studies (Reeves 2003), writing in every subject area was high on the list of the practices common to all these schools. The benefits of having students write were two-fold: first, it encouraged students to reflect and organize their thinking about what they had learned; second, it provided teachers with diagnostic information about their students' learning. And, although these schools often had to borrow time from other subject areas in order to put more emphasis on the language arts, their students actually improved in those other content areas. As Reeves puts it, "it is difficult to escape the conclusion that an emphasis on writing improvement has a significant impact on student test scores in other disciplines" (Reeves 2000, p. 190).

You can read more about asking better questions and helping students respond at https://hip-books.com/asking-effective-questions/.

Effective Instructional Strategies

Among the types of effective responses to reading, Graham and Hebert found that the lowly comprehension question rated high on the list. But there were two conditions for this practice to have optimal effect: first, teachers must ask good questions; and second, students must be taught how to write an effective response.

Robert Marzano (2001) has identified nine instructional strategies as "high-yield;" that is, those that generated the most significant gains in student performance across grade levels and subject areas. At the top of the list are Comparing/Contrasting and Summarizing.

Comparative thinking is a natural operation of our minds. From our earliest years, we learn by distinguishing one thing from another: foods we like and foods we don't, our family and everyone else, what is safe and what isn't. Teaching compare-and-contrast in school helps students build higher-level thinking skills, refine critical thinking, and understand the attributes and non-attributes of concepts. In literacy, we can compare characters, settings, plotlines, and even themes or messages.

Summarizing requires learners to analyze what they read, distill what is important, and consolidate the key details into "a shortened version of an original text, stating the main ideas and important details of the text with the same text structure and order of the original" (Kissner, 2006, p. 8). Our students are called upon to write summaries in many academic reading situations, from literature to textbooks to tests. But summarizing is not as easy as it sounds. Too many students write too much or too little, miss key details, or simply retell every detail, regardless of its importance. Part of the problem is that our students are often *assigned* to write summaries, but not as often *taught* to write them.

It takes a lot of practice for our students to be able to summarize effectively. We can start by having them practice orally, inviting students to talk to a partner about what happened in a recent television program, movie, or even video game in a minute or less. Point out that they didn't tell their partners every single line of the script, but chose just the important details to tell. That's what summarizing is all about.

Have students move on to practice summarizing short passages and then move on to larger sections of fiction and nonfiction text—chapters and even entire books. An alternative for students who have trouble distinguishing the key ideas from supporting details is to have them retell every detail of a familiar story, then condense those details into a summary by eliminating the unnecessary and finding ways to combine and categorize common details.

John Hattie, in his analysis of hundreds of studies of effective teaching practices (2009), placed "notetaking and other study skills" in the top ten "high impact" teaching strategies. Taking notes from a lecture, writing up a science experiment, summarizing a text, answering questions…there's nothing new about writing across content areas. But maybe the old is new again. Writing by hand with an old-fashioned pen and paper is a more effective way to take notes than using a computer! Researchers Pam Mueller and Daniel Oppenheimer (2014) found that note-taking with a pen, rather than a laptop, gives students a better grasp of the subject material. Why? In their study, students who took handwritten notes had to synthesize what they heard or read, while those working on a keyboard tended to copy the information verbatim.

> Try Twitter Summaries—tell about a reading passage in 140 characters!

Writing About Nonfiction Reading

Nonfiction reading requires all the skills and strategies that fiction reading requires—and more. The **WITIK Folder** is a note-taking protocol for before, during, and after reading. Based on the KWL charts of yore, WITIK is an acronym for "What I Think I Know" and invites students to access background knowledge before reading. Then, during and after reading, they note which of their WITIK facts were confirmed in the reading and add new learning, as well as identifying questions for further investigation.

Freewriting (also called quickwriting) is a time-honored writing warmup that involves writing nonstop for a period of time, writing whatever comes to mind and never lifting the pen from the paper. Sometimes writers are encouraged to just write nonsense or write the same word over and over until a new idea springs to mind. But I have found that too many students take advantage of this loophole and don't even try to write anything of substance, so I have them focus their freewrite on a specific topic of study. Give them a minute to think, then encourage them to write everything they know about the topic, unconstrained by correct grammar, punctuation, or sentence structure. Sometimes we have writers "loop" from one freewrite to another, choosing a word or phrase from the first task as the topic for the second. This is a great "exit slip" activity or a review of the day's (or the previous day's) learning or even an advance organizer (What do you already know?) about a topic.

Struggling Writers and Writing about Reading

Graham and Hebert (2010) found that writing about reading is particularly helpful for students who struggle—as long as their teachers provide plenty of instruction and guided practice in routines such as responding to questions, summarizing and taking notes.

Allow students to talk with a partner before writing; talking helps synthesize information and organize thinking, so they have more energy to devote to getting those ideas down on paper. Teach them to always "tell why" and consider the "three Es"—Elaboration, Explanation, and Evidence from the text. Most importantly, chill out on conventions. One of the biggest challenges for most of our struggling readers is managing the conventions of writing—spelling, punctuation, grammar, sentence structure. Here's where we have to consider our priorities. In a Writing Workshop, surface editing and correcting mechanics come at the last stage of a complete writing process, just before the work is published and shared with an audience. When it comes to "writing to learn," we need to back away from the "getting it right" and focus on the "getting it good"—which requires students to put words together to convey ideas with power and precision.

> **The Three E's of Effective Response:** Explanation, Elaboration, Evidence

MINILESSONS IN THIS CHAPTER

Lesson	Page	Learning Focus
The GIST and the 3E's	38	Writing good responses to reading
Write a Bad Response	39	Matching responses to a rubric
What's the Difference?	41	Comparing and contrasting in literature
Sum It Up!	42	Writing summaries of fictional passages
Focused Freewriting	44	Generating ideas
Chunk and Chew, Stop and Jot	45	Taking notes
WITIK: What I Think I Know	46	Recording ideas before, during, and after reading

The Gist and the Three E's

Learning Goal: Students will be able to respond to a question or prompt by providing an overview statement and offering Explanation, Evidence, and/or Examples from the text.

I DO: A good question or prompt will never be completely answered in just one sentence. It's hard to convince students that even if it looks like one sentence will do, they should always add more explanation. Display a simple prompt and response such as the one below.

Prompt: Who was the most important character in "Three Little Pigs"?

Response: *The wolf was the most important character in "The Three Little Pigs" because the pigs wouldn't have needed to build stronger houses if he hadn't been there. The pigs would probably have been quite happy in their houses of straw and sticks, but the wolf blew them down. That's why the third pig needed a strong house of bricks—to keep them safe from the wolf.*

The first sentence is what we call the "GIST," which stands for Good Introductory Statement. The word *gist* means the main point or general idea and that's what the GIST tells. But that's not all. A good response always tells more: some Explanation, Elaboration, and/or Evidence—the "Three Es"

WE DO: Write a collaborative response to a question such as, "Do you think wolves are treated fairly or unfairly in fairy tales?" Tell students to be sure to:

Start with a GIST that starts something like "I/We think wolves are
  - treated _____ because…"
  - Explain and Elaborate: give more information
  - Give Evidence from the stories, including specific examples.

YOU DO: Provide students with open-ended prompts from their own reading. Have them use the GIST and the 3 Es to structure their responses.

Write A Bad Response!

Learning Goal: Students will be able to identify an effective response and apply it in their own writing.

I DO: Sometimes the best way to learn how to write a good response is to start by analyzing a bad one! Show students some examples of extended responses at different levels of quality, such as the ones below.

> **In Jack in the Beanstalk, who is the villain and who is the hero? Why do you think so?**
>
> 1. Jack is the hero.
> 2. Jack is the hero and the giant is the villain because Jack is good, and the giant is bad.
> 3. The giant is the villain because he is mean and bloodthirsty. He threatens to eat Jack and drink his blood. Jack is the hero because he gets food for his mother.
> 4. Jack is really the villain because he broke into the giant's house and stole his magic hen and golden harp. The giant was only protecting his own property. There is no hero in this story because Jack was a thief and the giant threatened to kill Jack.

WE DO: Talk together about what makes some responses more or less effective than others. You might want to construct an anchor chart of criteria for an effective extended response. Better yet, build a rubric with your students, such as the one below:

NEEDS WORK	OKAY	GOOD	GREAT
The question might be partially answered, but it's not clear whether the writer really understood the passage or even read it.	The question is answered but without support from the text.	The question is answered with strong evidence from the text.	The answer is insightful and beyond the obvious, as well as well supported by the text.

As a group or in pairs, have students try to construct a Good or Great response to a question on a familiar text. A list of questions about common folk tales may be found on page 40. (Make sure that all your students are familiar with these stories, or select another one that you have read together.)

Alternatively, have students score a response such as the one below and work in teams to revise it to make it Good or Great.

> **Which character was most important to the story "The Three Little Pigs"?**
> I think the third pig was the most important because he was the smartest.

YOU DO: As you assign future prompts and comprehension questions, refer students to their rubrics or criteria for thorough, insightful, well-supported responses.

Try One of These!

1. What could Little Red Riding Hood have done to prevent the problems she had?
2. What should the three bears do with Goldilocks? What would be an appropriate punishment?
3. Who do you think was the villain in Jack and the Beanstalk, Jack or the giant?
4. Which of the fairy tale characters would you choose to be friends with?
5. Which of the three pigs was most important to the story? Why do you think so?
6. How did the pea show people that the girl was a princess? What would be a better test?
7. Can you think of a nonviolent way for the third billy goat to get across the bridge?
8. What is the lesson we should learn from Beauty and the Beast? Do you agree with it?
9. What is meant when someone says you are "crying wolf"?
10. Why did the witch choose to take away the Little Mermaid's voice? Why was this the most difficult thing for the mermaid?
11. In Rumpelstiltskin, who is the villain and who is the hero?
12. How would the story of Cinderella be the same and different if Cinderella was a boy?
13. How did the character _____ change from beginning to end?
14. What is the lesson we can learn from _____? How can we apply this lesson to real life?
15. How are the characters _____ and _____ alike and different?
16. Compare the settings of _____ and _____.

What's the Difference?

Comparing and Contrasting is considered to be one of the most effective learning strategies. This lesson teaches a simple foldable graphic organizer based on the Venn Diagram to use for comparing characters in a story, but it could easily be adapted to comparing settings, plots and even themes.

Learning Goal: Students will be able to identify the similarities and differences between two characters in literature.

I DO: Remind students of the importance of understanding characters in literature. Tell them that this is a simple graphic organizer that will help them to identify things that are similar and things that are different about two characters. Demonstrate how to create the foldable and complete the front folds by naming and/or illustrating each character. Unfold and write two or three unique features of each character and use the center portion to identify common characteristics.

WE DO: Instead of (or as well as) modeling the entire organizer, you might identify two familiar characters from their reading and have the students suggest characteristics to add to each section.

YOU DO: Have the students choose two characters and create their own organizer.

Note that this graphic organizer may be used for comparing characters, settings, plot lines, or even themes. Vary the size of the paper for interest and to indicate how much writing is expected.

INSTRUCTIONS FOR MAKING A COMPARE AND CONTRAST FOLDABLE:
1. Fold a piece of paper in half.
2. Fold each edge in toward the middle to form "shutters".
3. Use the outside flaps to identify the character differences and the inside flaps to identify the character similarities.

Sum It Up!

Learning Goal: Students will be able to effectively summarize a piece of fiction or nonfiction reading.

I DO: Talk with students about ways that we use summarizing all the time. You might ask a student to tell what the weather is like today. Of course, they don't recite the entire weather report; they *summarize* it by saying, it's sunny and hot or it's windy or it's raining. Remind students that when they summarize, they tell the most important parts, in a shorter version of the original.

Display the passage "Trouble in Grade Five" (page 43) or another passage of your choice and model and think aloud as you create a summary.

WE DO: Ask the students to help you identify the most important ideas in the passage:

- *The character was rinsing paintbrushes in the sink and couldn't turn the faucet off.*
- *There was a fire in the school and everyone had to leave.*
- *When they came back, there was water everywhere.*

Use a shared writing approach (the group composes the text together and the teacher scribes), construct a summary of the key ideas. You might come up with something like this:

The main character is cleaning paintbrushes in the sink when the fire alarm goes off. He can't turn the faucet off, but he has to go out of the school with the other kids. It turns out that there's a real fire and the tap was running the whole time. It caused a flood and he was in trouble.

YOU DO: Remind the students of the Seven Rules for Summarizing. Provide another simple passage for them to summarize individually or in pairs.

Seven Rules for Summarizing:

1. Make sure to include all information that is important.
2. Leave out information that might be interesting, but not important to the main part of the story.
3. Put the details in the same order in which they appear in the text.
4. Don't repeat information, even if it's repeated in the text.
5. Use key important words from the text when you can.
6. Combine ideas or events that go together.
7. Use category words instead of lists of individual words.

Trouble in Grade Five

Back in Grade Five, I was rinsing some paint brushes in the sink when the fire alarm went off. I told Mrs. P. that I couldn't turn the faucet off, but she ignored me, so I just lined up with the other kids and we all marched outside in single file.

That would have been no problem if it had been a fire *alarm*. But it wasn't. It was the real thing.

Some garbage container in the boiler room had gone up in flames. Before long, the fire engines arrived, sirens screaming, and we all watched the firemen go rushing in. In Grade 5, that's big excitement.

By the time they came out, it was nearly three o'clock, so the principal dismissed us. I confess — I forgot all about the faucet.

I never did see the actual flood. Some kids say that the water from the coatroom had turned into a tidal wave. Other kids say that water was spurting out the windows and doors of our classroom. I don't know which is true. All I know that there was water everywhere by the time I got to school. And I was in serious trouble.

Excerpt from *One Crazy Night* by Paul Kropp

Focused Freewriting

Learning Goal: Students will be able to generate several details on a topic using the freewriting strategy.

I DO: Introduce the concept of freewriting: writing as many details, facts, or ideas on a topic as possible within a limited time frame, without worrying about spelling or conventions. Encourage students to spell words so they can read them (because no one else will be reading them) and punctuate if they feel like it. The main thing is for them to put down as many ideas as they can—and be able to read those ideas later. Outline the basic rules for freewriting (below). You might want to create an example to help illustrate the process.

FOUR RULES FOR FREEWRITING

1. You can't **not** write. Even if you can't think of anything related to the topic (and you will be able to, of course), write about anything at all. Don't lift your pen from the paper (or your fingers from the keyboard) until the time is up.
2. Forward motion only. Don't go back and erase, cross out, or change what you've written. Don't even take time to reread. You can do that when the time is up.
3. Feel free to piggyback on ideas that you've already written; in other words, go off in a different direction.
4. If you want to use punctuation, do. If you don't want to, don't. Spell words as well as you can, as long as you can read them. Write long sentences or short sentences or no sentences at all. The main point is free flowing ideas.

WE DO: Use a guided writing approach to practice using focused freewriting to review a lesson or topic of study. Give the students a topic and tell them that they will have one minute to write nonstop. Provide a curriculum-related topic and tell the students you will set the timer for one minute. They must write nonstop about that topic until the time is up.

When the timer sounds, all students must put down their writing instruments, even if they're in the middle of a word. Have them read over what they've written, then circle one word or phrase that will be the topic for another one-minute freewrite. We call this a "loop." Set the timer for another minute and have students repeat the process to see how many more ideas they can add to the topic. Sometimes, I will have them count the words they've written during the first loop and try to "beat their record" on the second. Much to their surprise, they almost always do!

YOU DO: Have students turn and talk to a partner about what they've written. They don't need to share their writing, but simply tell their partners what they remembered about the topic. It's an interesting exercise to compare which facts about a topic both partners recalled, and which ones were unique to one partner or the other.

> A one-minute time frame is a good starting point for intermediate students. Most will be easily able to write for a minute, so it will build success. If everyone seems to be writing diligently, increase the time for a few seconds, but, ideally you want the students to run out of time before they run out of ideas.

Chunk and Chew, Stop and Jot

This lesson works well for taking notes from a visual presentation. You might want to combine it with the lesson on Telegram Notes (page 56).

Learning Goal: Students will be able to summarize chunks of information that they hear.

I DO: Not everything our students learn is from print. Tell students you are going to read or tell them some information about a topic or show a video. Their job is to watch, listen, and learn. Tell students that they will be asked every few minutes to "stop and jot"—to write down what they learned.

WE DO: Read or view for a short time, then pause at a strategic spot for students to mentally "chew" on what they've heard. At the stopping point, give the students one minute to write down what they remember. (Alternatively, have them do a one-minute freewrite, as on page 44.) As the students "chew" on the information, you might want to have them talk to a partner before and/or after they write. Continue this with more "chunks" of information to build the habit of writing notes to summarize information that they hear and/or see.

YOU DO: Have students Turn and Talk to a partner about what they recalled from the teaching. Did they miss any key ideas? Did they have any misconceptions? Encourage them to reflect on whether/how their writing helped them understand and remember.

WITIK — What I Think I Know

Based on the KWL chart, this graphic organizer helps students gather information before, during and after reading. Model using a large sheet of tag board or chart paper, but later students can have individual WITIK charts created from file folders.

(Note that introducing the WITIK chart might be a minilesson, but completing all parts of the folder will take place over a series of lessons. After completing the chart, there are many things you can do with the sticky facts on the "confirmed" and "learned" charts. Have students sort them into categories or use them to write a summary of the passage.)

Learning Goal: Students will be able to access background knowledge, gather information, and reflect on wonderings before, during, and after nonfiction reading.

I DO: Create a large WITIK folder by folding a sheet of tag board or chart paper in half. Label the four sections as follows:

- WITIK (What I Think I Know)
- CONFIRMED!
- LEARNED
- WONDER?

Tell students that it's a good habit to think about what they already know about a topic before they start reading about it. Sometimes we already know a lot and sometimes we "sort-of" know some things. WITIK stands for "What I Think I Know" and the WITIK chart is a tool for brainstorming some things we think we might know about a topic.

Select a nonfiction text to read aloud or together. Before reading, think about the topic of the text and show students how you generate some ideas you already know and some you think you know. Invite them to add their ideas, and record all of them on sticky notes. Tell students to think as they read about which of the WITIK facts on the chart are confirmed in the reading.

WE DO: Read the text aloud or enlarge it to read it together as a shared reading process. After reading, invite students to identify which of the WITIK facts were confirmed in the reading. Move the respective sticky notes from the WITIK section of the folder to the "CONFIRMED" section inside the folder. Later, revisit the text to add facts to the "What I Learned" section and questions to the "What I Wonder" section. Otherwise, save this routine for another lesson.

YOU DO: Provide students with their own WITIK folders. You might create labels or simply have the students label their own. Laminating the folders will make them a little more durable for multiple uses, but it is not essential.

Chapter 4   Writing to Inform

Ancient Egypt

The life of an average child in Ancient Egypt was very different from modern life. They had schools, pets and homes, but they were a lot different. There was a smaller variety of pets, but some were very unusual. Childhood did not last as long as it does today.

Egyptian childhood was nothing like modern childhood. If you were an Egyptian child, you'd be running around without clothes on most of the time! And what about hairdos? Boys had a plait that was on the right side of their heads and the rest of the head was shaved.

School was also harder. Children went to school at a young age. But if you were a girl, at age 12 you would have to stay home. Students used either plastered board or stone to write on (just like on the Flintstones). If a child was not listening, they might be beaten.

Animals played a part in ancient Egyptian life. Your family pet was probably a dog, cat or monkey. To show their love for their cat, people would shave off their eyebrows when it died!

If you were an ancient Egyptian, you would eat mostly vegetables. Richer people enjoyed beef and poultry, especially goose. But people thought that fish and pork were not clean.

As you can see, the life of an Egyptian child was quite interesting, but I think I would rather live today.

It's happened more times than I care to count. I have instructed my students to write a research report—on a country, a planet, a famous person in history, or various other topics—only to be disappointed when they handed in a sheaf of papers that were little more than a collection of snippets copied from a website.

Researching and reporting have always been ubiquitous assignments in intermediate classrooms, and never more than today, when inquiry-based learning is playing an increasingly important role in our curricula. The Writing Next report cites **inquiry activities** as one of the most effective elements of writing instruction (Graham & Perin, 2007). And while the five-paragraph essay may have gone the way of the dinosaur, there is still a need for the skills of searching, sifting, and sorting information and communicating that information in clear and coherent written form. Teachers might choose to have students present their learning in a range of multimedia formats, but the traditional research report, with carefully selected facts, logical organization, complete sentences, and conventional spelling, still holds a revered place in the worlds of college and career.

There are few places where the symbiotic relationship between reading and writing is more evident than in accessing informational text. Informational writing structures help students to organize their thinking in ways that are different from narrative story structures. Students must read in order to gather information for writing. They need to mentally sift and sort to select the information that is relevant to their purposes. They must learn the unique structures of informational text, negotiating not just the print but also the visuals, such as pictures, charts, tables, and graphs. And they need to use organizers, such as tables of contents, indexes, and glossaries. At the same time that students are creating informational text, they are improving their ability to read it.

The research report must be taught, just like any other text form. Whether the writing task is part of a science, social studies, visual arts, or language arts class, students need explicit instruction in how to gather information and present it in a coherent and well-crafted written form. And following a process from conception to publication is just as important as it is with narrative text. This unit takes writers through the whole the writing process: prewriting—choosing a topic and gathering information; drafting—putting the notes in sentences and paragraphs; revising—making those sentences and paragraphs even more interesting and powerful; and editing/publishing—polishing the writing to make it accessible to a reader.

Although this chapter could be the framework of a complete unit on research writing, you might want to include additional lessons to meet the requirements of your own class and curriculum. Alternatively, this chapter can offer a menu of lesson ideas from which you may pick and choose to supplement your own program. As always, I urge users of this book to adapt the minilessons to suit their needs and classroom circumstances.

Many of the lessons in this chapter introduce fairly complex writing tasks, such as taking notes, developing research questions, and writing topic sentences, any of which may require more attention than one brief minilesson. As always, assessment of student progress should guide the pacing, presentation, and lesson sequence.

One of the challenges of teaching a unit such as this is that writers complete various stages of the process at different rates and times. Because the structure of the unit can be somewhat "lock-step," students should be encouraged to work on writing projects of their choice when they complete the genre tasks of the day. Remember that you're never done Writing Workshop!

An Informational Writing Unit of Study

FEATURES OF INFORMATIONAL WRITING	LEARNING GOALS Students will be able to:	MINILESSONS *lesson is found in this book

The content is focused on rich and specific details around a topic, usually beyond the existing knowledge of the writer.
 	
The information is grouped into subtopics or subcategories of the main theme.
 	
Interesting details, varied sentences, and engaging voice hold the reader's interest.
	• Choose a topic and narrow it down to a specific aspect or feature of the topic.
	• Conduct external research to inform readers about the topic.
	• Organize the body of the piece, putting facts together that belong together.
	• Use writer's techniques to capture and hold a reader's attention.
	• Craft opening and closing paragraphs that introduce and summarize the main theme.
	• Use technical vocabulary appropriate to the topic.
		1. *Skinny Down the Topic
		   Explaining "why it matters"
		2. *Telegram Note-taking
		   Gathering information without plagiarizing
		3. *Terrific Topic Sentences
		   Organizing information by subtopic
		4. *Book-End Paragraphs
		   Openings and closings
		5. *Gems to Make Writing Sparkle
		   Writer's techniques to add voice and tone
		6. *The First Four Words

TEACHING AN INFORMATIONAL WRITING UNIT

<table>
<tr><td>

Steps in Teaching an Informational Writing Unit

1. Analyze examples.
2. Choose and focus the topic.
3. Determine subtopics or research questions.
4. Collect information on the topics.
5. Draft the report in sentences and paragraphs.
6. Compose opening and closing paragraphs.
7. Revise for clarity and craft.
8. Polish to publish.

</td></tr>
</table>

1. Analyze examples of the text form.

When teaching a unit on any genre or text form, I always start by providing students with opportunities to read and analyze both professional and student examples. In our book *The Write Genre* (2004), Paul Kropp and I recommend "immersing students in the genre" to ensure that they understand the structure of the texts they are about to write. Today, there are myriad examples of good informational writing for intermediates, from picture books to magazines (print and online) such as *National Geographic Explorer* and *Time for Kids*.

It's always a good idea to keep an ongoing collection of good examples on hand, both professional and student-written, such as the fifth-grade piece "Life in Ancient Egypt" at the beginning of this chapter. Invite the students to read several examples of the text form and construct an anchor chart of common features of the text form using guided questions such as:

- What do you notice about the topic and details?
- What do you notice about how the paragraphs are organized?
- What do you notice about the opening and closing?
- What do you notice about the personality, tone, and style of the piece?
- What writer's techniques or special words did the writer use?

2. Choose a topic and focus on it.

Choosing a topic isn't difficult. Deciding what matters about this topic is a little harder. A common problem for many writers is choosing topics that are too broad. "All About Spiders" might be a great topic for a first-grader, but in upper-level writing, it tends to get unwieldy, unfocused, and uninteresting. We want more than a laundry list of facts on a general topic, we want to know: What's your point? What makes this topic interesting? Why should readers care? Sometimes we don't know what the point or main idea of our piece is until we do a little research. By taking time to **Skinny Down the Topic**, writers will find it easier to focus both their information-gathering and their writing.

3. Decide on subtopics and create a gathering grid to collect notes.

It's an expectation that intermediate students will conduct some research for their reports. You might have a student who thinks he knows everything there is to know about skateboarding or peregrine falcons, but he should be encouraged to search for something he didn't know. Some writers will take longer than others to figure out their main point or "thesis."

Then it's time to zero in on two or three subtopics to research. Some writers might have just two subtopics and others might have five or six; it really depends on the topic. We often add the ubiquitous "Other Interesting Facts" for information that doesn't fit into our subtopics, but we just might find a place for it somewhere. (Hang on to those fascinating facts for gems to make the writing sparkle!) Identifying subtopics helps writers organize their ideas and avoid rambling on with a collection of random facts that are tied together only loosely, if at all.

A Gathering Grid such as the example on page 53 is a great tool for collecting facts on a topic. Ideally, enlarging it to 11"x17" provides lots of room for writing. You can reproduce the graphic organizer on page 53, but it's easier and quicker to simply fold the page in four, then four again (to make 16 squares). Students can also use the back of the sheet for additional subtopics. Each subtopic should generate at least three or four facts—enough to form a paragraph of connected text. Students should also be encouraged to record the sources of their information, from websites to print resources to human experts.

4. Gather information.

How do you get students to collect information from sources without plagiarizing large chunks of text? I like to draw an analogy to good old-fashioned telegrams, where every word costs money. You had to distill your message into only the most important words, just as you do when you take notes. **Telegram Notes** provide modeling and practice in taking jot notes on a topic.

Start by preparing Gathering Grids with the subtopics recorded across the top row. In the boxes below each topic, the student records facts about that subtopic. In the column on the left, the student records the source of those facts. Of course, this means that they might need a lesson on how to find resources. Most of our intermediate students are capable of searching the worldwide web, but some might need guidance in choosing appropriate (and reader-friendly) websites.

You'll need to decide what bibliographic information you want students to include and teach them to record that information. For intermediate students, I find it sufficient to record the author, title, and publication date or website name and URL. I generally require the students to use at least two sources, perhaps one print and one online.

As they research, they should write notes on the section of the grid that corresponds to each subtopic and source, being judicious in the choice and quantity of words they use to record "just the facts."

Don't forget the Bibliography: author, title, and publication date or website name and url.

5. Transfer the notes into a rough draft with sentences and paragraphs.

When the writer is satisfied that she has collected enough information, she's ready to transform those notes into connected text; what we call the "first draft." The great advantage to the gathering grid is that the information is already organized by subtopic. Usually, the notes for each research question or topic will form one paragraph; now the writer needs to focus on crafting interesting sentences with those notes. Model, model, model! Take time to demonstrate how to turn those bulleted notes into flowing sentences.

As we show students how to compose a draft, we also want to model using a voice that speaks to a reader and conveys the information in an interesting and engaging style. We used to think that informational text should be as dusty as a dictionary. However, the old rules have fallen by the wayside in today's informational writing. We want informational text to be every bit as rich and engaging as this newspaper weather report:

> From British Columbia through to Manitoba, Old Man Winter balled up his fist Wednesday and delivered a roundhouse white-knuckled wallop of wicked winds and towering drifts that were blamed for at least two deaths and gridlock on roads and at airports. — *Globe & Mail*, January 11, 2007

Four or five facts on each subtopic will lend themselves perfectly to paragraphing, even if the piece is only one-page long. (And it really shouldn't be much longer.) Loathe as I am to revive the anachronistic "hamburger paragraph," (commonly described as a topic sentence, three details, and a wrap-up sentence) three details do work quite neatly. But that doesn't rule out four details or even two. Let's face it, some paragraphs will have two details, others will have twenty; it just depends on the writer, the topic, and the text. And, as far as topic sentences are concerned, they usually appear at the beginning of a paragraph or occasionally may appear at the end or buried in the middle, but they are never repeated at the beginning and the end of the paragraph in any kind of writing.

What about topic sentences, anyway? Back in 1975, a researcher named Richard Braddock reported that only about 13% of expository paragraphs opened with explicit topic sentences—and cautioned teachers and textbooks not to teach them. However, others disagree, and I find that **Terrific Topic Sentences** can be very useful structures for helping intermediate writers organize their writing.

6. Craft opening and closing paragraphs.

I usually encourage students to draft the body of the piece first, then add the introduction and conclusion, the **Bookend Paragraphs** on either end. The opening paragraph should grab the reader's attention and make him want to read more. The ending usually summarizes or reiterates the main point, sort of an "all-in-all" statement.

7. Revise for clarity and craft.

The rough draft is done! Now it's time to "re-view" the text and revise it for clarity and power. It's always important to start by making sure that the content makes sense and all the pertinent information is in place. Peer conferences (page 100) can help with this. Have students read their rough drafts to a partner and invite the partner to ask questions or point out confusing or incomplete information.

Informational writing, like all writing, should have a flair and style that speaks to a reader. Open an issue of *Owl*, *Sports Illustrated*, or any other magazine, and you'll see lively informational writing that sparkles with style as well as interesting content to capture the reader's attention. Amazing facts, quotes, questions, comparisons, and anecdotes are just some of the **Gems that Make Writing Sparkle**.

When writing sounds bland and monotonous, it's often because of a lack of variety in both words and sentences. How do you avoid using the same words over and over and over when you're talking about a single topic? One solution is to have the students highlight words that appear more than two or three times in their writing and then try to find synonymous words or phrases to replace them. Sentence after sentence that is the same length and structure makes writing sound choppy and mechanical. **The First Four Words: Making Your Sentences Flow** helps writers attend to the rhythm and cadence of the text by revising sentence beginnings.

8. Polish to publish.

Of course, before any piece of writing is taken to publication, we must get out that editing cloth and polish up the conventions. You will want to build minilessons on spelling patterns, punctuation, capitalization, subject–verb agreement, etc. into this unit. Use your local curriculum and your own assessments of your students' strengths and weaknesses to determine which lessons—and expectations—are appropriate at this point.

Most modern informational text is full of photographs and other visuals. You might want to offer additional minilessons about how to organize a word-processed page, how to find and insert visuals, and how to create organizers such as a Table of Contents, Index, Bibliography, and Glossary.

Ultimately, what we want is for our students to build long-term strategies for choosing relevant topics, collecting data, and sharing what they've learned in text that is interesting and engaging for a reader. Carefully planned lessons that demonstrate the processes of informational writing are the best antidote for pirated papers and tired text.

Subtopic Gathering Grid

	SUBTOPIC 1	SUBTOPIC 2	SUBTOPIC 3
SOURCE 1			
SOURCE 2			
SOURCE 3			

Pembroke Publishers © 2018 *Marvelous Minilessons for Teaching Intermediate Writing, Grades 3–8* by Lori Jamison Rog ISBN 978-1-55138-329-3

MINILESSONS IN THIS CHAPTER

Minilesson Title	Page	Learning Goal
Skinny Down the Topic	55	Finding the focus
Telegram Notes	56	Gathering information without plagiarizing
Terrific Topic Sentences	58	Organizing information by subtopic
Bookend Paragraphs	60	Crafting effective openings and closings
Gems to Make Writing Sparkle	62	Writer's techniques to add voice and flair
The First Four Words	64	Varying sentence beginnings

Skinny Down the Topic

Skinny Down the Topic makes research more focused and writing more manageable. It also limits the length of the piece. Student writing should be long enough to express the key ideas but short enough to maintain quality and interest. Two or three hundred words (about two hand-written pages) are enough for an intermediate-grade report.

Learning Goal: Students will be able to select and focus a topic for research and writing.

I DO: I tell students that I was asked to write an informational piece about Amusement Parks. That's a pretty big topic! There are many amusement parks in the world and lots to do at every one of them. In Kindergarten or Grade 1, you could call your writing, "All About Amusement Parks", write two or three details and consider yourself done. In upper grades, "all about" a topic might take a hundred pages, and even then, you might not be done. And it often becomes is like a grocery list of facts, instead of an interesting piece of writing that readers will want to read. The key to good informational writing is deciding the "so what?" What is the message or theme that I want to create about that topic? What might my reader be interested in reading? I wasn't sure what I wanted to say about Amusement Parks until I did some research. Then I decided I would write about the two main reasons people go to Amusement Parks: for the food and for the rides, especially the roller coasters.

WE DO: Choose a broad topic that students will know quite a bit about and collaborate to come up with some suggested focus topics. For example, I thought I might write about "Chocolate." Not only is that a big topic, but, "so what?" The students might come up with ideas like:

- Why people like chocolate so much.
- How chocolate is made.
- How chocolate was discovered.
- What you can make with chocolate.

YOU DO: You might want to have students generate a topic list from which to choose, or link the research report to a content area study. Have students choose a broad topic and do some research to "skinny it down." Tell them to think about what they could say about that topic in about one page or maybe two. Have them talk to a partner about their topics and what they plan to focus on.

Telegram Notes

What if every word you wrote cost money? That's the premise of this lesson on gathering point-form notes on a topic. Teaching students to gather research using jot notes is particularly important in this "cut-and-paste" generation. And it's quite a difficult skill. Take plenty of time to practice in large and small groups before expecting students to take jot notes on their own. The short-term pain is worth the long-term gain in control over copying. For students who are just learning note-taking, I find it helpful to have them hand in their notes for teacher review before starting to draft the connected piece.

Learning Goal: Students will be able to use point-form notes to gather and organize information about a topic.

An internet search will turn up many examples of famous telegrams, including the message from Orville Wright to his father describing the world's first airplane flight: (https://www.wdl.org/en/item/11372/).

I DO: Explain to students that in the olden days, when people needed to get a message quickly to someone far away, they used telegrams. You needed to go to a special office where someone with a special machine could send the message. Needless to say, it was very expensive. Because every word cost money, people were very careful to use only the words they needed to convey the message clearly. Words like *the* or *a*, for example, were often left out.

When we gather information to write an informational report, it's a little like writing a telegram. We can't copy every word from someone else's writing; we have to pick and choose our words carefully, so we just write the important fact without using any extra words.

Use the attached article on "The World's Favorite Flavor" to model for students how to gather information by writing point form notes. For example:

- *500 years ago—only cocoa powder from beans*
- *Cocoa powder—bitter taste, turns mouth brown*

WE DO: With the students, read a nonfiction article such as "The World's Favorite Flavor" (page 57). Go through some (or all) of the article, sentence by sentence, noting which sentences have relevant facts and using an interactive writing process to generate telegram notes.

YOU DO: Have students begin collecting notes on their own research topics. It's useful to have created a Gathering Grid (page 53) for students to organize their notes and record their sources. Remind the students to write only the words they need in order to understand and remember the fact when they revisit it later.

Rules for Telegram Notes:

- Write each fact on its own line, starting with a dot or "bullet".
- Use only key words.
- Don't worry about complete sentences or punctuation.
- Think about each word as costing money. How could you keep your note as inexpensive as possible, while still ensuring that you'll remember what the note is about?

The World's Favorite Flavor

What's the world's favorite flavor? If you guessed chocolate, you're right. In fact, the average American eats over 11 pounds of chocolate a year! From a tree in the rain forest to the sweet sauce on your ice cream, the story of chocolate is a fascinating one.

Five hundred years ago, hardly anyone in the world had tasted chocolate. Before that, people only had cocoa, which is a powder made from beans that grow on a tree called a cacao. But cocoa beans do not taste good by themselves. They are bitter and turn your mouth brown.

It wasn't until the 1500s that people in Europe learned how to turn cocoa into chocolate. They shelled, roasted, and crushed the cocoa beans to make cocoa butter. Then, they heated the cocoa butter to make a thick paste called chocolate liquor. In 1875, Swiss chocolate makers added milk and sugar to liquid chocolate. That was the first milk chocolate. Today, it's the most popular kind of chocolate.

In 1847, the J.S. Fry Company in England poured chocolate into square molds. These were the first chocolate bars. But they were bitter and not very popular. In the 1890s the American candy maker Hershey made bars from milk chocolate. Everyone loved them.

Chocolate has come a long way from its beginnings as a bitter-tasting bean. Today, there are over 30,000 kinds of chocolate candies to satisfy your sweet tooth. And if that's not enough, there is chocolate toothpaste, chocolate pasta, and even chocolate soap! Every day, all over the world, people are enjoying the world's favorite flavor.

Pembroke Publishers © 2018 *Marvelous Minilessons for Teaching Intermediate Writing, Grades 3–8* by Lori Jamison Rog ISBN 978-1-55138-329-3

Terrific Topic Sentences

Teaching students to use a gathering grid for note-taking helps them organize information as they collect it. Usually the notes on each subtopic neatly align themselves into paragraphs. Topic sentences also help students organize their thinking in paragraphs.

Learning Goal: Students will be able to craft informational paragraphs with topic sentences.

I DO: Share a writing sample that contains a clear topic sentence, such as the paragraph about penguins below:

> Penguins can't fly but they can move in other ways. Instead of wings, they have flippers that help them swim. On land, the penguins use their tails and flippers to help them balance. Penguins either waddle on their feet or slide on their bellies across the snow. This is called "tobogganning."

Notice that the first sentence in this paragraph tells what the rest of the paragraph is about. That's why it's called a "topic sentence". You can sometimes find topic sentences at the end of a paragraph and sometimes buried in the middle. But most often it's the first sentence in the paragraph. (Note that it is never repeated at the beginning and end of a paragraph.)

WE DO: When we're creating a first draft, we can put all the facts under each subtopic in one paragraph. Sometimes we create the topic sentence as we're drafting, and sometimes we create the topic sentence after we've written the rest of the paragraph. Read the following paragraph together and have students work in pairs to craft a topic sentence.

You might come up with something like, "Frogs and toads may seem similar but there are many differences between them."

If you feel your students need more practice in crafting topic sentences, reproduce the blackline master on page 59 and have them work in groups to create a topic sentence for each paragraph.

> Frogs have bulging eyes, smooth or slimy skin, and strong webbed hind feet. They prefer warm, moist environments. Toads, on the other hand, have dry, warty skin and stubby bodies with short hind legs. That's because toads move by walking instead of hopping, as frogs do.

YOU DO: As students begin writing the first drafts of their informational pieces, encourage them to use paragraphs for each subtopic, beginning each paragraph with a topic sentence. You might consider having students plan a topic sentence for each subtopic right in their gathering grids.

Terrific Topic Sentences

I don't know which part I like the most: the scary costumes, the carved pumpkins, or the candy, candy, candy! Every year, I plan my costume months ahead. On the big night, my friends and I dash from door to door, filling our bags with treats till their almost too heavy to carry. Sometimes we even play a trick or two, but it's all in fun.

Mozart began to play the harpsichord when he was only three years old. By the age of five, he had composed his first piece of music. When he was six, he performed concerts for the King and Queen of Austria. Before long, he was giving concerts all over Europe.

Always swim with a buddy. If one of you gets tired, or gets in trouble in the water, the other can get help. Only swim in places that you know. If you can, stick to places with a lifeguard. Make sure the water is deep enough before you dive. Know your limits and watch out for one another.

Pembroke Publishers © 2018 *Marvelous Minilessons for Teaching Intermediate Writing, Grades 3–8* by Lori Jamison Rog ISBN 978-1-55138-329-3

Bookend Paragraphs

*The "bookends" are the opening and closing paragraphs of the piece, often crafted after the body of the piece is done. You might choose to teach the introduction and conclusion as two separate minilessons. See page 78, **AIM for a Great Opening** for a lesson on introductory paragraphs.*

Learning Goal: Students will be able to craft effective opening and closing sentences/paragraphs for their informational reports.

I DO: You might want to bring in a picture or an actual set of bookends to show students how they hold a collection of books together. In the same way, the beginning and ending of a piece of writing hold the details in the body together. Read or display the opening paragraph from "World's Favorite Flavor" (page 57).

Talk to the students about what the writer has done in this paragraph. It starts with a question to grab the reader's attention. Then it offers an amazing fact (with an exclamation, just to remind readers how amazing it is!). The last sentence in the paragraph introduces readers to what they're going to read in the rest of the piece.

In this lesson, or as a separate lesson, review the closing paragraph for the same piece. Again, talk about what the writer has done: reviews the main idea, adds a "gem" (fascinating fact) and repeats a key phrase—"favourite flavour"—from the opening paragraph. In most informational writing, the closing paragraph includes a summary of the thesis or key point of the piece—an "all-in-all" statement.

WE DO: You might want to send students on a hunt for examples of good bookend paragraphs in informational books and articles. Have students write their examples on large sheets of chart paper ("graffiti board") and display them for others to read.

With the students, collaboratively craft bookend paragraphs for another piece of writing, such as the reproducible on "Penguins" on page 61.

YOU DO: As students work on creating opening and closing paragraphs for their writing, some may need additional support. You may want to provide students with some possible sentence stems for a general statement, as shown below.

Suggested sentence stems for opening or closing paragraphs:

- It's hard to believe it, but...
- You'll soon discover that...
- There are many reasons that...
- You may be surprised to learn that...
- It's interesting that...
- Let's take a look at...
- As you can see,...
- Most people would agree that...
- It's clear that...
- Clearly,...

Penguins

Penguins live in the southern hemisphere. About ten percent of penguins live in Antarctica, the coldest place in the world.

Penguins can't fly but they can move in other ways. Instead of wings, they have flippers that help them swim. On land, the penguins use their tails and flippers to help them balance. Penguins either waddle on their feet or slide on their bellies across the snow. This is called "tobogganning."

The female penguin lays the egg, then she goes off to find food for the baby. The male takes care of the egg while she is gone. The male holds the egg on his feet and tucks it under his feathers to keep it warm until it hatches. When the female comes back, they take turns looking after the chick.

Pembroke Publishers © 2018 *Marvelous Minilessons for Teaching Intermediate Writing, Grades 3–8* by Lori Jamison Rog ISBN 978-1-55138-329-3

Gems to Make Writing Sparkle

This lesson invites students to identify writers' techniques and to try these techniques in their own writing. A list of ideas is provided at the end of this lesson, but it's better to construct your own chart, introducing a few at a time as you gradually build a repertoire of "gems" to make writing sparkle.

Learning Goal: Students will be able to identify and apply a range of writer's techniques to add voice and style to informational writing.

Literature Link: In titles like *The Human Body*, author Seymour Simon has used a range of literary techniques to make informational writing sparkle with voice.

I DO: Seymour Simon's book *The Human Body* is full of paragraphs like this: *"Your body has about 100 trillion cells. That's 100 followed by 12 zeroes! If you were to count one cell a second nonstop, you would need millions of years to count a single trillion cells!"* (page 6).

Read this or another text like it to show students how nonfiction text can be full of excitement and voice. Invite the students to note three techniques that Seymour Simon has used: an amazing fact, a couple of exclamations, and a comparison to help us fathom this huge number. These techniques are like the "bling" that authors use to make their writing sparkle with personality.

Create an anchor chart of "Gems that Make Writing Sparkle" and gradually add to it as you and the students discover more writer's techniques to enhance nonfiction writing.

WE DO: Remind the students that now they know three writer's techniques to make their nonfiction writing sparkle: fascinating facts, exclamations, and comparisons. Work together to revise a piece of text like Penguins (page 61) to add each of these features. You might come up with something like:

Most penguins live in Antarctica, the coldest place in the world. Imagine living in a place where the average temperature is 50 degrees below zero! That's at least five times colder than the freezer on your fridge at home.

YOU DO: Have students try to revise their own informational writing to include a fascinating fact, an exclamation, and a comparison. Note that "gems" don't always need to be added after the fact. Often they arise naturally in the drafting of the piece. That's where that category of "Other Interesting Facts" on the gathering grid can be useful.

GEMS to Make Informational Writing Sparkle

- A fascinating fact or statistic

- An interesting comparison

- A question

- A simile or metaphor

- Alliteration

- An exclamation

- A quote from an expert

- An example

- An anecdote or story

- Something funny

- A personal connection

- A very short sentence or sentence fragment

- A sensory description

Pembroke Publishers © 2018 *Marvelous Minilessons for Teaching Intermediate Writing, Grades 3–8* by Lori Jamison Rog ISBN 978-1-55138-329-3

The First Four Words

A lot of informational writing suffers from "same sentence structure syndrome": Penguins are... Penguins have... Penguins can... Here are some techniques to avoid "subject-verb" tedium by varying the first four words of each sentence.

Learning Goal: Students will be able to revise their sentence beginnings to add variety and fluency.

I DO: Display these two sample paragraphs from early drafts of "The World's Favorite Flavor" and read them out loud. Notice that the first one sounds a lot smoother and more interesting than the second because the sentences are more varied. Highlight the first four words in each sentence and note that all the sentences in the second paragraph start with "The ___ are." When sentences are all the same length and begin the same way, the writing tends to sound choppy.

<table>
<tr>
<td>

Five hundred years ago, hardly anyone in the world had tasted chocolate. Before that, people only had cocoa, which is a powder made from beans that grow on a tree called a cacao. But cocoa beans do not taste good by themselves. They are bitter and turn your mouth brown.

</td>
<td>

The cacao beans are roasted and crushed to make chocolate. The pods are shelled and the inner seed is crushed so it turns into cocoa butter. The butter is then heated to make a thick paste called chocolate liquor, even though it doesn't contain alcohol.

</td>
</tr>
</table>

WE DO: Use a shared writing approach to collaboratively revise the second paragraph of the chocolate piece. You don't have to change every sentence; just enough to add fluency. You might come up with something like:

Can you believe that these bitter cocoa beans can turn into sweet chocolate? First, the pods are shelled, and the inner seed is crushed. Now you've got cocoa butter! Then the butter is heated to make a thick paste. Although it doesn't contain alcohol, this paste is called chocolate liquor.

YOU DO: Have students highlight the first four words in each sentence in one of their drafts and revise as necessary to add variety to some of the sentences. They don't have to change *every* sentence; just every second or third one so they don't all start in the same way.

Ways to vary your sentence beginnings:

- Flipping the sentence to change the order of the phrases
- Starting with a when or where (prepositional phrase)
- Starting with a "how" (adverb) or "what kind" (adjective)
- Starting with an "ing" word (verb)
- Starting with a "traffic light" (transition) word

Rubric for Assessment & Evaluation

The following rubric is based on the lesson goals described in this chapter.

	GREAT		GOOD		NEEDS WORK
CONTENT	The topic is clear and focused with plenty of rich facts. Details are organized by subtopic, in paragraphs with topic sentences. A strong opening grabs the reader's attention and the closing wraps the piece up neatly.		The piece is full of interesting facts. Details are organized by subtopic, with some attempt at paragraphing. There is an effort at crafting an opening and closing paragraphs.		The facts are limited, disjointed or mundane, perhaps because the topic is too broad. There is no attempt at paragraphing. There are no opening and/or closing paragraphs.
CRAFT	The voice is lively and will keep a reader interested. The writer has used "gems" to add voice and interest. Varied sentence beginnings and lengths make the piece sound pleasant to the ear.		The voice sounds "friendly" but pretty much all the same. There are a few writer's techniques ("gems"). There is some sentence variety but most sentences are similar in structure and length.		This writing sounds a bit like the dictionary—just the facts. There are few or ineffective writer's techniques. There is no variety of sentence structure at all.
CONVENTIONS	Almost no errors in spelling and mechanics.		Few errors in spelling and mechanics.		Many errors in spelling and mechanics make the writing hard to read.

Chapter 5   Writing to Persuade

> I believe teachers shouldn't give detentions when kids are late! I have three good reasons why. First, sometimes teachers are late, and they just walk in like nothing happened and say, "Sorry I'm late." Then when we come in late they say, "I will see you at lunch." or, "Why are you so late?" That's not fair, and it's a double standard. Second, detentions are a huge waste of time. For example, if you are done everything and you get a detention for being late, you have to sit in an empty room for 15 minutes. Fifteen minutes doesn't sound like much. But it is if you are not doing anything. Third, my sister is really, really slow and my mom and dad make me wait for her, so she makes me late. Therefore, when I'm late because of her, it's really not my fault! For all of these reasons, I believe teachers should not give detentions because we are late.

Our students are no strangers to the powers of persuasion! Every time they plead with the teacher to lighten their homework load, or beg for that expensive pair of name-brand sneakers, our students are using persuasion. If there's any doubt about how pervasive persuasion is in our society, we have only to look at the number of words we have in English to describe the action of trying to bring someone around to your point of view, such as *coax, cajole, convince, entice, entreat, exhort, impel, influence, inveigle, persuade, prevail upon, reason, seduce, sell, sway, talk into, turn on to, wear down, wheedle, win over,* and *woo!*

This is a great age and stage to get students writing about issues that are important to them in their school lives, their home lives and the wider world. Topics that matter are the foundation of passionate persuasion.

Even in primary grades children can learn to state an opinion and provide reasons for it. However, we want intermediate students to expand basic opinion writing into more sophisticated persuasive writing. They must learn not just to state their opinions, but also to rationalize their opinions with a reader in mind. Consideration of audience is one of the key differences between simple opinion writing and effective persuasive writing. This ability to step outside of oneself and see the argument from the point of view of someone else is a big challenge for young writers.

Furthermore, it's no longer enough to support an opinion with an opinion. "I like summer because I like to play outside in the sun" might be acceptable for an emergent writer, but the fluent writer in intermediate grades needs to provide both reason and rationale. An organizational structure such as "**What, Why, and How Do You Know?**" encourages young writers to support their thinking with facts and statistics.

When young writers have a real-life purpose and audience, they not only write with more voice and power, but research has shown that they are also more willing to revise and edit their writing to make it even more passionate and powerful. Perhaps they might try to persuade fellow students to reduce the amount of garbage in the lunchroom at school. Maybe they can convince the principal to organize a staggered recess period to allow for sharing of limited playground equipment. One group of intermediate students successfully lobbied their city council to construct an accessible playground in a nearby park.

There are many ways to convey an argument to an audience, especially in today's multi-media world: PowerPoints and podcasts, blogs and vlogs, Twitter feeds, Instagram posts, and so on, with new social media tools cropping up all the time. Is teaching a traditional persuasive essay a little passé?

Perhaps there will be a not-too-distant future in which complete sentences, standard spelling, and rhetorical devices don't matter. But, in today's world, the written word still reigns supreme in formal persuasion. Furthermore, persuasive writing helps students learn to reason, to think logically and rationally, and to convey their ideas to others using conventions of language that are understood and accepted by all. It encourages writers to view issues from another point-of-view and to communicate with clarity and purpose. And finally, it helps young people understand and interpret the advertising and other persuasive print with which all of us are constantly bombarded. As Barry Lane and Gretchen Bernabei (2001) assert in their book *Why We Must Run with Scissors*, teaching the persuasive essay teaches students "to have opinions, to be passionate about these opinions and to defend them with strong, well thought-out and elaborated arguments" (p. 1). And, may I add, to communicate those arguments to someone else in a way that the reader will understand and be swayed.

Persuasive writing can help students make a difference in their world. At age nine, Severn Cullis-Suzuki and some friends started the Environmental Children's Organization, and at age 12, she gave a powerful speech to the United Nations Earth Summit in Rio de Janeiro. Craig Kielburger was only 12 years old when he read an article about child labor and gathered a group of kids to found Free the Children. Severn and Craig not only took on a cause, but also persuaded others to join them. All over the world, teens and preteens are making a difference in the world. Your students could do the same.

A Persuasive Writing Unit of Study

PERSUASIVE TEXT FEATURES	LEARNING GOALS Students will be able to:	MINILESSONS *Lesson is found in this book
Content focused on opinions that the writer feels strongly about, with reasons and evidence to support the opinion. Evidence often includes facts, examples, statistics, and quotes from experts. Writing is organized with an opening that states the opinion, a body that outlines the reasons and support for the main point, and a conclusion that restates the opinion. Voice is clear and passionate and directed to a specific audience. The writer deliberately uses words that pack an emotional punch and often uses the words *I, you, and me.*	• Choose a topic that reflects an opinion that they care about. • Gear the writer's voice, word choice and content to a reader. • Provide solid reasons to justify the opinion. • Conduct research for examples and information to support the reasons. • Organize the body of the piece logically with reasons and support. • Craft an opening that grabs the reader's attention and states the main point. • Craft an ending that restates the opinion and offers a "call to action." • Consider word choice that speaks to the audience and is intended to generate an emotional response.	1. *Agree or Disagree** Topic chart to help generate opinions and choose topics 2. *What, Why, and How do you Know?** Planning and organizing details 3. *Face the Facts** Conducting research 4. *Other People Might Say** Considering other points of view 5. **Putting it all together** Considering the order of the reasons and support 6. *Loaded Words** Word choice that packs an emotional punch 7. *AIM for a Great Opening** Crafting an opening that includes an Attention Grabber, Background Information, and Main Point. 8. *End with an I, You, or We** Concluding with a call to action

TEACHING A PERSUASIVE WRITING UNIT

Steps in Teaching a Persuasive Writing Unit

1. Read and analyze samples of the text form.
2. Identify topic and audience.
3. Make a plan for developing the argument.
4. Gather evidence to support arguments.
5. Anticipate and refute the argument.
6. Compose a rough draft.
7. Create opening and closing paragraphs.
8. Revise for word choice and sentence fluency.
9. Polish to publish.

1. Read and analyze samples of the genre.

Children's magazines such as *Time for Kids* and *Scholastic Scope* are excellent sources for age-appropriate persuasive and opinion writing. There are many engaging picture books that feature persuasion, but they tend not to be structured in the traditional format. It's always a good idea to keep an ongoing collection of good examples (especially student samples) on hand, such as the sixth-grade piece "I Hate Detentions" at the beginning of this chapter. Invite the students to read some examples and discuss the common features of the text form, using guiding questions such as:

- What do you notice about the topic and details?
- What do you notice about how the writing is organized?
- What do you notice about the opening and closing paragraphs?
- What do you notice about the personality and style of the piece?
- What writer's techniques or special words did the writer use to add voice?

As we read examples of the text form, we collaboratively construct a framework organized around the structure, organization, and language of that form. The framework in the table on page 27 is provided for teacher background, but you will want to guide students in using their own words.

2. Identify the topic and audience for the writing.

There are many ways to generate topics for persuasive writing. Brainstorm a list of issues that concern intermediate students. Ask them what they would change if they could about rules at home, at school, and in the world. **Agree or Disagree** uses a graphic organizer to identify issues of concern to the students that might inspire a piece of persuasive text. The reproducible on page 73 contains a number of suggested issues, but you will want to add or substitute issues of specific interest to your students.

In truth, the topic itself is less important than the way it's developed. And finding real causes to write about engages and empowers young writers and may lead to more purposeful writing to authentic audiences, from parents to principals to politicians.

More than any other type of writing, persuasive text is directed toward a specific audience. Before starting a piece of persuasive writing, writers must ask themselves questions such as: Whom am I trying to persuade? What words and ideas do I need to use in order to convince this reader to think the way I do? What arguments might make this reader agree with me?

> When writers have a meaningful topic, an authentic audience, and a clear purpose, they will write with more passion and voice, and be more concerned about clarity and conventions.

Some people believe that intermediate students are unable to decenter their writing, taking the focus off of themselves and placing it on their reader. But Gail Tompkins (2012) asserts that, "when students have a clear purpose and plausible reason for writing, they can adapt their writing to meet the needs of their readers" (p. 353). When writers have a meaningful topic, an authentic audience, and a clear purpose, they will write with more passion and voice, and be more concerned about clarity and conventions. You may want to use the minilesson **TAP Into Voice** (page 104) to teach students about identifying topic, audience, and purpose for any text.

3. Make a plan that develops the argument with reasons and explanations.

Unlike narrative and informational text, persuasive writing is organized around reasons and explanations for a thesis or strong opinion. In school, we have often taught the persuasive piece as a formula: State the opinion, offer three reasons, and restate the opinion. As we see in the sample piece on Detentions, rigid formulas can generate decent, but rarely great, writing. Having a framework for writing can help students gain control of a new form, but might limit their continuing growth as writers. In truth, some issues require three reasons, others may have far more, and yet others may need only one compelling argument.

A more flexible, but still supportive structure for developing an argument is the **What, Why, and How Do You Know** planner. This organizer asks writers to state their opinions (what?), articulate reasons for their opinions (why?), and find evidence to support those reasons (how do you know?).

4. Conduct research to collect evidence to support your opinion.

The "how do you know?" part of an argument often requires writers to do some research to locate external support. Sophisticated writers know that opinions aren't effectively supported by other opinions, particularly their own! You might want to revisit **Telegram Notes** (page 56) to guide students in conducting research for facts, statistics, examples, and quotes from experts to back up their opinions in writing.

Literature Link: Karen Orloff's picture book *I Wanna Iguana* is a delightful example of point and counterpoint.

5. Anticipate and refute the argument.

The most sophisticated element of persuasive writing is anticipating—and rebutting—potential opposition to one's argument. As challenging as it is to tailor one's argument to an external reader, it is even more difficult to try to anticipate the other person's counterargument. **Other People Might Say...** (page 77) teaches writers to anticipate a reader's opposition and offer additional support for their own arguments.

6. Turn the plan into a draft.

A strong plan always makes drafting easier. **What, Why, and How do you Know?** provides a good foundation for arguments and support. Students can use this material to draft the body of the piece, adding the opening and closing paragraphs later. There is no consensus about how to order the arguments; some say to put the strongest point first, while others say to close with the most important point. In the end, the order of the arguments is up to the writer.

Many intermediate students struggle with making the transition from a plan to a draft. As always, teacher modeling and demonstration are the best tools we have for helping students through the composition stage.

Good persuasive writing (and, for that matter, any writing) is full of energy and personality (also known as "voice"). It's difficult to add voice after the fact, so students should be encouraged to consider voice and tone as they draft. Simply choosing an opinion the author feels strongly about is often enough to generate passionate writing. However, there are a few tricks that writers use to appeal to their reader. Using the words, *I, you*, and *we* invites readers to be part of the campaign. A sprinkling of questions, exclamations, and even commands (See **Three Sentence Stories,** page 126) also draws a reader in.

7. Add introductory and concluding paragraphs.

When the body of a piece is complete, writers can tackle the opening and closing paragraphs. In the traditional argumentative structure, the opening paragraph states the premise or thesis, and the closing paragraph summarizes the argument. When we add an engaging lead and a satisfying ending, we have a well-crafted persuasive piece. **AIM for a Great Opening** teaches students three parts to a strong opening paragraph: Grab the reader's *attention*, provide some background *information*, and clearly state the *main point*. Usually, the concluding paragraph reiterates the key point and ends with a call to action—an *I, you, or we* statement.

8. Revise for word choice and sentence fluency.

After completing the draft, students will need to revisit, review, and revise their piece of writing for clarity and voice. This is the time to consider whether the language and tone of the writing speaks effectively to a reader. Well-chosen vocabulary can contribute significantly to persuading someone else to agree with our point of view. **Loaded Words** teaches students to purposefully use words that generate emotional responses above and beyond the words' intended meanings (Engel, 2000). Loaded words elicit a response—positive or negative—from a reader. For example, the noun *plant* generally carries no emotional baggage, whereas *rose* usually inspires a positive reaction, and *weed* carries a negative connotation. That's why advertisers like to use words like *new, improved, best*. Judicious use of loaded words in persuasive writing can help influence a reader to come around to our way of thinking.

9. Polish and publish.

Once the writing says what the writer wants it to say, in the way the writer wants to say it, the piece may be edited and polished for publication. The publication of persuasive writing can take many forms, from a letter to an editorial. As always, an authentic audience is the best incentive for powerful writing, in any form.

MINILESSONS IN THIS CHAPTER

Lesson Name	Page	Strategy
Agree or Disagree?	72	Generating topics based on strong opinions
What, Why, and How Do You Know?	74	Planning and organizing arguments
Face the Facts	76	Conducting research to support arguments
Other People Might Say…	77	Considering other points of view
AIM for a Great Opening	78	Crafting an effective opening paragraph
End with an I, You, or We	79	Concluding with a call to action
Loaded Words	80	Using words that pack an emotional punch

Agree or Disagree?

When writers choose topics they feel strongly about, it's much easier to draft and craft the piece of writing. The reproducible on page 73 suggests several topics for intermediate students, but you and your students will want to add, delete, or substitute ideas that are of relevance to them.

Learning Goal: Students will be able to identify topics for writing that they strongly agree or disagree with.

I DO: Tell the students that good persuasive writing starts with a topic that the writer cares deeply about. Today, they will have the opportunity to consider a number of issues and how they feel personally about those issues. Display the reproducible on page 73 or a similar set of issues, and think aloud as you consider how you would respond to the first few and how to record your responses on a Likert-type scale. Discuss the differences between "mildly agree" and "strongly agree." Invite your students to add or change some issues of interest to them.

WE DO: Provide each student with a copy of the adapted "Agree or Disagree Chart" on page 73. Read the first opinion, then have students run their fingers across the page to note each of the levels of response, putting a checkmark or X in the column that best reflects the strength of their opinion. If you're not sure your students will be able to read the statements, or are concerned that they don't know how to complete a chart such as this, read some or all of it together, with each student marking his or her own chart.

YOU DO: After the students have completed their charts, tell them to highlight the opinions that have a checkmark under the "strongly agree" or "strongly disagree" columns. Tell them that these are the opinions that will make the best persuasive writing because they are the ones the writers care most strongly about. Invite students to meet with a partner and discuss their highlighted topics. This will help them decide which issues they have the most to say about.

Agree or Disagree?

Opinions	Strongly Agree	Mildly Agree	Don't Agree or Disagree	Mildly Disagree	Strongly Disagree
Girls and boys should be in separate classes in school.					
Kids should be allowed to have cell phones at school.					
Computers don't really help kids learn.					
There should be no homework on weekends.					
Kids should be able to bring junk food for lunch.					
Every classroom should have recycling bins.					
School should start at 10:00.					
Kids in Grade __ should have longer recesses.					

_____

_____

_____

_____

_____

Pembroke Publishers © 2018 *Marvelous Minilessons for Teaching Intermediate Writing, Grades 3–8* by Lori Jamison Rog ISBN 978-1-55138-329-3

What, Why, and How Do You Know?

This is a terrific organizer for intermediate students and definitely merits more than one minilesson. Encourage students to try completing more than one planner on different topics, so they solidify their understanding of how to use this organizer and also so they can find the one that lends itself to the strongest argument.

Learning Goal: Students will be able to plan and organize persuasive writing by stating an opinion, providing reasons for that opinion, and offering evidence to support those reasons.

I DO: Remind students that good persuasive writing doesn't just give an opinion—a "what." It has to provide a few good reasons for that opinion—the "why." But if you really want to convince your reader, you should also give some evidence behind those reasons; in other words, the "how do you know?" Read together a text such as "I Hate Detentions" (page 66) and identify the reasons and support for those reasons (see example on the left).

WE DO: Choose a topic of interest and invite students to work together to begin a planner. For example, we might choose the common topic: "Our school needs to have a Litter-free Lunchroom policy." This is a good topic to work with because most students can identify with the issue and it lends itself to conducting some research. Invite the students to come up with some reasons why a Litter-free Lunchroom is a good idea. They are likely to generate a couple of good reasons and, if pressed, a few not-so-great ones. Focus on the quality of the ideas, not the quantity. Weak or illogical reasons weaken an argument rather than strengthening it.

But what about the third column—"How do you know?" It's quite possible—probable, in fact—that students won't have the evidence to support their reasons. The next minilesson, **Face the Facts,** addresses this issue.

> **Deconstructing "I HATE DETENTIONS" (page 66)**
>
> **What?** Kids shouldn't have detentions when they're late for school.
>
> **Why?** It's not fair and it's a double-standard.
>
> **How do you know?** Often teachers are often late and they think it's okay.

> Somewhere along the line, we've gotten the idea that there must be "three reasons" to support an opinion. In truth, there might be only one or two solid reasons. Or there might be four or five. Remember that a few good reasons are more important than many marginal ones.

What?	Why?	How do you know?
Our school should implement a litter-free lunchroom policy.	We produce too much garbage every day. Throw-away packaging is wasteful and expensive.	??

YOU DO: Now it's the students' turn to select a topic they feel strongly about. Provide each student with a copy of the **What, Why & How Do You Know?** graphic organizer (or teach them to fold a piece of paper in three) to start identifying their opinions and reasons. If they know some evidence, they can add it to the third column or start researching facts to support their argument.

What, Why & How Do You Know?

What? (Opinion or Main Point)	Why? (Reasons for Opinion)	How do you know? (Evidence to Support Reasons)

Other people might say …

_____

_____

_____

But I say …

_____

_____

_____

Pembroke Publishers © 2018 *Marvelous Minilessons for Teaching Intermediate Writing, Grades 3–8* by Lori Jamison Rog ISBN 978-1-55138-329-3

Face the Facts

A good argument is supported by evidence: facts and statistics beyond the writer's personal opinion. In this lesson, students learn to find research support for their thesis.

Learning Goal: Students will be able to research facts, examples, and statistics to support their opinions and reasons.

I DO: Share a partially completed **What, Why & How Do You Know?** chart, such as the example below.

What?	Why?	How do you know?
People shouldn't use so much bottled water.	It's damaging to the environment.	

Share the following two pieces of support for the "Why" statement:

- *"It's messy when people litter."*
- *"Fewer than 20% of plastic bottles in the United States are recycled. The rest fill up landfills, taking hundreds of years to decompose."*

Talk about the difference between the two statements. The first is just another opinion, whereas the second is a fact; it's a special kind of fact called a statistic because it involves numbers. Elicit from students that the strongest evidence ("how do you know?") comes from facts and specific examples.

For some students, it might be necessary to clarify the concept of "specific." To say that Americans buy a lot of bottled water is a generality; to say that they buy about 30 billion bottles of water every year is a specific fact. It's important to avoid words like "lots" or "many" or "some" and replace them with actual numbers. Usually, we have to conduct research or consult experts in order to find these specific facts, statistics, and examples.

WE DO: Revisit the group's **What, Why & How Do You Know** chart from the previous lesson and discuss how we might find factual evidence to support our reasons why we should have a Litter-free Lunchroom. You might come up with something like:

What?	Why?	How do you know?
Our school should implement a litter-free lunchroom policy.	We would eliminate a lot of garbage.	*According to wastefreelunch.org, every school-age child generates about 67 pounds of waste per year.*
	Throw-away packaging is wasteful and expensive.	*A typical disposable lunch costs about $4 a day while a waste-free lunch costs about $2.65—a savings of almost $500 over the school year.*

YOU DO: Have students access print and online sources to research facts and statistics to insert into their individual **What, Why & How Do You Know?** planners.

> Depending on the extent of research teachers want their students to conduct, they might want to revisit the **Telegram Notes** minilesson on page 56. It's always a good practice to have students use more than one source and to cite the sources of their information.

> Check out the website www.wastefreelunches.org for a kid-friendly (with no advertising) website full of examples and statistics.

Other People Might Say...

Anticipating and countering an opposing argument requires sophisticated conceptual thinking. Not all of our intermediate writers will be able to step outside of themselves enough to think from the reader's perspective.

Learning Goal: Students will be able to develop and counter a possible argument against their stated opinion or thesis.

I DO: Revisit the importance of gearing our persuasive writing to a reader. One of the hardest things about persuasive writing is trying to predict what our reader will be thinking. Sometimes we need to guess reasons why readers might disagree with our opinions and try to offer evidence against their arguments before they even argue with us! Anticipating the reader's opposition—and arguing against it—gives the writer a head start in persuading the reader.

Share your thoughts aloud so that students can see the thought process involved with deciding how to organize their writing. For example, "In my persuasive piece, I think I've got some pretty good arguments about why people should stop using bottled water. I have some facts and statistics about the cost of bottled water and how plastic is harming the environment. But, I also know that some people believe that bottled water is healthier than tap water. So, when I did some research, I found that tap water in most North American cities is more carefully monitored for bacteria than most bottled water. In fact, much of the water we buy in bottles is actually just tap water."

WE DO: In the group piece, there are some good arguments in favor of Litter-Free Lunchrooms. Why don't more schools do it, then? What arguments might people have against it? Together, come up with some ideas about why people might disagree, mainly convenience and time. Then they can brainstorm some arguments against this idea. You might come up with something like this:

> **Other people might say...** that using disposable packages saves time for busy families.
>
> **But I say...** getting in the habit of filling reusable containers becomes quicker over time. Plus, isn't it worth a few extra minutes to save your family money and protect the environment?

YOU DO: Have students add **Other People Might Say...But I Say...** to their individual **What, Why & How Do You Know?** planners.

"AIM" For a Great Opening

Learning Goal: Students will be able to craft an effective introduction that grabs the reader's attention and states the main thesis or opinion.

A—Attention grabber
I—Background Information
M —Main Point

I DO: Tell students that in persuasive writing, it's important to let readers know the writer's position right from the start. But any good opening statement first has to get the reader's attention. Display the following paragraph:

Try to picture 30 BILLION plastic bottles. That's how many bottles of water Americans buy EVERY YEAR! And three-quarters of those bottles will end up in landfills— or in the oceans. That's why I think we should stop using disposable water bottles.

Draw students' attention to the amazing fact in the first sentence, designed to grab the reader's attention. (The next two sentences provide some background information and the last sentence clearly states the writer's opinion — and what the rest of the piece will be about.) We use the acronym AIM to remind us about the Attention Grabber, Background Information, and Main Point or opinion in a good opening paragraph.

There are many ways to hook a reader. You might want to revisit the minilesson on **Gems to Make Writing Sparkle** for inspiration.)

WE DO: Together, craft an **AIM Opening** for the group piece on Litter-free Lunchrooms. Have the students brainstorm ideas for grabbing a reader's attention. A question often works well. Maybe the statistic on how much garbage each student produces each year? They already know the main point. What piece of information might tie the two sentences together? You might come up with something like this:

A — **Attention Grabber:** *Can you believe that the average student in a school lunchroom produces about 65 pounds of garbage a year?*
I — **Background Information**: *But we can reduce that to almost zero by eliminating disposable packaging.*
M — **Main Point:** *It's time to consider a litter-free lunchroom policy at school.*

For younger or less sophisticated writers, you might want to consider teaching just the Attention Grabber and Main Point.

YOU DO: Have students use AIM (or AM — Attention Grabber and Main Point) to craft an opening paragraph for their persuasive writing pieces.

End With I, You, or We

Persuasive writing often ends with a "call to action" — something I, you or we can do.

Learning Goal: Students will be able to craft an effective closing paragraph that calls for action from the writer, the reader, or both.

I DO: Remind students that a good ending in persuasive writing wraps the piece up neatly and leaves the reader both understanding and (you hope) agreeing with your point of view. Often, a good way to end is by calling for some action that the writer, the reader, or both can or should do. We call that an **I, You, or We** statement. Display the conclusion to the sample piece on Bottled Water (page 81) as an example of a call to action.

WE DO: Collaboratively craft an **I, You, or We** ending for the group piece on Litter-free Lunchrooms. You might come up with something like: *So start saving those margarine tubs and yogurt containers to reuse for packing school lunches. The earth will thank you.*

YOU DO: Have students craft an **I, You, or We** closing for their individual pieces of persuasive writing.

Loaded Words

Why is it that some words pack more of an emotional punch than others? Looking for loaded words in reading can be quite a fascinating educational routine. Often readers don't even know that they're being "manipulated" by a writer. You might want to take this lesson into the reading block and have students examine a piece of advertising or a brochure from a tourist attraction. Ask them to note words that are intended to make a reader want to buy that product or go to that place. They're likely to find words like fun, exciting, family, *and even* free. *You might even initiate a discussion about how certain words might be positive for some readers and negative for others (such as a "wild and woolly roller coaster ride").*

Learning Goal: Students will be able to identify and use words that are meant to make readers feel a certain way about a topic.

I DO: When we write to try to persuade someone to think the way we do about an issue, we usually focus on the ideas and reasons for our thinking. But did you know that the words we use can also make a reader feel a certain way about an issue? For example, using words like "healthy" or "safe" typically cause a positive reaction from most people. Words like "germs" or "caution" tend to cause a negative reaction. We call these "loaded words" because they can create emotions or feelings. Often, we use loaded words automatically, without even thinking about them. But it's important to pay attention to the way that the words we use influence our readers.

WE DO: Display the finished piece on bottled water on page 81. Have students identify any loaded words or phrases they notice, and categorize them as "positive" or "negative." (There are no right or wrong answers here. Any word or phrase that elicits an emotional reaction in a reader is a loaded word for that reader.) Talk about some loaded words we could use in a piece on Litter-free Lunchrooms.

YOU DO: Have students examine their own persuasive writing drafts and highlight any loaded words they have used. Encourage them to revise their writing by inserting or substituting at least two words or groups of words for more effective persuasion.

> Another writer's technique for persuasive writing (and speaking) is **The Magic of Three** (page 107).

Try to picture 30 *billion* plastic bottles. That's five times as many bottles as there are people in the entire world. And that's how many bottles of water North Americans buy *every year*. Unfortunately, most of those bottles will end up in landfills or the ocean. This is just one of the reasons why I think it's time to stop using plastic water bottles.

Bottled water is damaging to the environment. Less than 20% of plastic bottles are recycled. The rest fill up landfills, taking hundreds of years to decompose. Scientists report that there is an island of discarded plastic in the Pacific Ocean that is more than twice the size of Texas.

Bottled water is also really expensive. A bottle of water can cost up to $2 or more, while tap water costs almost nothing. In fact, bottled water costs more than gasoline! Most of that money doesn't pay for the water itself. It's for packaging, advertising, and selling. We spend over $15 billion a year on bottled water—and that's over and above what we've already paid in taxes for our own tap water.

Some people argue that bottled water is healthier and tastes better than tap water. Actually, much of the water that we buy in bottles is really just tap water! Sometimes it has been purified, but not always. In some ways, tap water is even better for you. For example, many cities add fluoride to tap water to prevent cavities and tooth decay. In most places, tap water is more carefully checked for bacteria than bottled water is. But does it taste better? Showtime Television gave people in New York a hidden taste test of bottled versus tap water, and 75% of them actually preferred the taste of the tap water!

So the next time you want to take a drink to the beach, on a run, or for a ride in the car, grab a reusable bottle and fill it from the kitchen tap. You'll be doing some good for your body, your wallet, and the earth.

Rubric for Assessment & Evaluation

The following rubric is based on the lesson goals described in this chapter.

	GREAT		GOOD		NEEDS WORK
CONTENT	The opinion or main point is clear and well supported with reasons and evidence. An "AIM" opening grabs the reader's attention and the "I, You, or Me" closing wraps the piece up neatly.		The opinion or main point is clear with some reasons and evidence. There is an effort at crafting an opening and closing		The opinion or main point may or may not be clear but it is not well supported. The opening and/or closing are incomplete.
CRAFT	The writing is full of passion that speaks to a reader. The writer has effectively used techniques such as loaded words.		The writer seems to care about the topic and tries to convince the reader. The writer has used some loaded words.		The writing isn't convincing. The writer doesn't seem to care about the topic. There aren't many special words to convince a reader.
CONVENTIONS	Almost no errors in spelling and mechanics.		Few errors in spelling and mechanics.		Many errors in spelling and mechanics make the writing hard to read.

Chapter 6   Content Minilessons: Topics and Details

> **My Memory**
>
> I have a lot of memories but my favorite memory was my trip to Disneyland. My whole family had a blast. The rides, the shows and meeting all the characters was so fun. But my favorite ride was Splash Mountain. First I would wait in line full of excitement. Then I would get in a log with butterflies in my stomach and then ride through the story. Soon I would go up the hill and all of a sudden I went whooshing down with the water splashing in my face and frogs jumping in my stomach. It was so much fun and that's probably why I went on it five times! I loved that trip and it's a memory I'll never forget.

Beethoven took four famous notes (*da-da-da-DAH*) and turned them into the *Fifth Symphony*. Michelangelo started with another artist's unfinished statue and ended up with one of the most iconic sculptures of all time. E.B. White was wandering through an orchard on the way to a pigpen when he saw a spider web—and the rest is history. Whether it's in art, music, or the written word, creating involves taking a basic idea and extending, expanding, enriching, embellishing, and refining it.

Too many of our intermediate students produce narratives that are little more than "breakfast to bed" stories—lists of chronological details without development, all receiving the same amount of attention and importance. Instead, we want our students to focus their topics and elaborate on key details, as the fourth-grade author did in the memoir at the beginning of this chapter. Instead of reciting a laundry list of activities at Disneyland, she focused on one thing: Splash Mountain. Then she not only explained what happened on the ride, she also described her feelings throughout. That's what elaboration is all about.

Every piece of writing starts with a topic—an idea or theme or message. If writers are going to care about their writing, they've got to care about their topics. So we're not doing them any favors by assigning topics or prompts. Save the prompts for content-area writing, when students need to respond to a piece of literature or log a science experiment or document their thinking in mathematics. It may seem counterintuitive, but the more students write—and the more they write about their own choices—the easier it will be for them to come up with topics for writing. Ask any professional writer and they will tell you that they have more ideas than they'll ever be able to use. The more you write, the more you see the world as a writer.

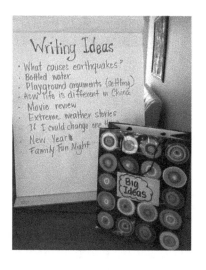

The "Big Ideas" Bag

Here's a solution for "I don't know what to write about" Syndrome.

Keep an ongoing list of potential topics for writing, based on classroom events or studies: what causes earthquakes, how to solve arguments on the playground, the best part of Family Fun Night, fracturing a fairy tale, how to score a goal in hockey. All the topics should be related to shared classroom experiences; you don't have to go to Disneyland to have something to write about. In this way, students have a constant reference point if they're struggling for a topic.

I try to add three or four topics every day, but the chart soon fills up, so I cut up the chart and put the separate topics into a large gift bag (hence the "Big Ideas Bag"). If a student is really stuck for a topic, he or she has the option of drawing a random topic out of the bag. The catch is—they must write about the topic they've drawn.

Writing is all about topics and details. Writers need to select the details that will enhance their composition, and then elaborate on those details to bring them to life. Even a great story can be lost on a reader if details are missing or out of place.

Elaboration involves clarifying and expanding on ideas to send a message to the reader about which ones are the most important and interesting. It can slow down the reading to build suspense or take the reader galloping on a whirlwind of excitement. Writers have many strategies for elaborating on details, including the "golden rule of writing:" Don't tell me, show me!

As teachers, we often advise students to "tell me more" or "add more details." However, simply adding more words to a piece of writing doesn't necessarily make it better. How can we teach students how to take a seed of an idea and develop it into a powerful and interesting message? How can we help them learn to discriminate between the relevant detail and the extraneous one? And how can we help them build the strategies writers use to bring those details to life? That's what the minilessons in this chapter are about.

MINILESSONS IN THIS CHAPTER

Lesson Title	Page	Learning Focus
Topic Bingo	86	Generating topics for writing
Trifold Planner	88	Producing and organizing details
Listing or Layering	91	Elaborating by adding supporting details
Don't Tell Me, Show Me!	93	Elaboration using show, don't tell
Add an Anecdote	95	Elaborating with examples
Slo-Mo Writing	96	Slowing down the writing to make it more exciting
Dabble in Dialogue	97	Elaborating with short bits of dialogue
Stars and Wishes	100	Peer conferences

Topic Bingo

We want our students to come up with their own topics for writing. But we don't want them to waste precious writing time trying to think of something to write about. Topic generating activities like this one scaffold students in generating a list of topics that are still their own, and available to them when needed. You will notice that all of the sentence stems on this Topic Bingo Card lend themselves to Personal Narrative writing; however, it's very easy to create stems for other text forms as well. Students keep their Topic Bingo Cards in their writing folders to use as needed.

Learning Goal: Students will be able to generate a collection of potential topics for writing.

I DO: Display the "Bingo Card" organizer on page 87 and think aloud as you complete several of the sentence stems. This is an opportunity to show students that sometimes it's easy to come up with ideas and sometimes it's more difficult.

WE DO: Give each student a copy of the Bingo Card to complete the sentence stems with their own experiences. We call it a Bingo Card, not just because of the grid configuration, but because we try to write something in every square. Allow enough time for everyone to get at least part of the card completed; some might have to use workshop time to finish.

YOU DO: Tell students that the middle square is for an idea from another writer. Give them time to share one story from their card with others in a group. Maybe they will get an inspiration from one of their partners. Once they've told their stories, they should be ready to start writing them. No one can say, "I don't know what to write" because they all have a ready-to-use collection of their own ideas at their fingertips.

Leave the center square blank for students to add an idea of their own or "get an idea from another writer."

Topic Bingo Card

I had a great time when…	I was really angry when…	It wasn't fair when…
I did something nice for someone when…		I laughed so hard when…
I got this scar when…	I learned my lesson when…	I was really sad when…

Pembroke Publishers © 2018 *Marvelous Minilessons for Teaching Intermediate Writing, Grades 3–8* by Lori Jamison Rog ISBN 978-1-55138-329-3

Trifold Planner

A strong prewriting plan helps the writer shape the piece of writing. It reminds the writer to think about how to grab the reader's attention at the outset, what details to include and in what order, and how wrap the piece up neatly.

Teaching this prewriting tool has been broken down into three lessons to keep them short and not take away from independent writing time. The third component, planning an opening and closing, is for more sophisticated writers, and it might even be taught at a later time. Of course, as always, teachers may choose to alter, combine, or omit parts of this lesson to suit the needs of their students.

Students should complete at least three or four trifold planners before turning any into a draft. This gives them practice in using this strategy to plan narrative story structure and add details and elaboration. When students have had adequate practice completing this planner, take time to explicitly teach them how to turn their plans into connected drafts. Use one of your models to show students how you consider the order of the details, how you will structure them into sentences, and what you might add that isn't in the planner. Then follow the same process with a collaborative text before requiring students to complete their own drafts.

MINILESSON 1

Learning Goal: Students will be able to plan details for the beginning, middle, and end of a writing piece.

I DO: Review what students know about the structure of personal narrative stories (i.e., details and elaboration told in chronological order). Tell students that they will learn a simple organizer for planning the beginning, middle, and end of a piece of writing, using a "trifold" (a fancy word for a paper folded in three). You can use the reproducible on page 90 or teach students to fold a piece of paper into three horizontal sections and two vertical sections.

Model using a three-column organizer, on paper or on screen. Choose a topic of personal interest (from the Bingo card, for example) and demonstrate how you might summarize the beginning, middle, and end of a narrative—only a sentence or two for each. Plan ahead what you will write and say—but think aloud for the students as though you are composing it in your mind.

Invite your writing partners (the students) to ask you questions about each section. Tell them that this helps you as a writer decide what key details readers will want to know. As time permits, start adding details to each section, beginning, middle and ending. Add words or phrases you might want to use in any section. (These might be complete sentences, but don't have to be.) This section of the lesson might wait for another day.

WE DO: Choose a shared event and have the students work collaboratively to summarize the beginning, middle and end. Record their ideas on a three-column organizer.

YOU DO: Have students select a topic from their **Topic Bingo** cards. Provide each student with a trifold planner (or the equivalent on word processor) and ask them to plan a beginning, middle, and end for their personal narrative. You might want to have them talk through their narrative with a partner before summarizing the beginning, middle, and end.

Tip for folding a piece of paper in three:

Cut strips of cardboard the exact width of a third of the page and have students use them as templates for folding.

MINILESSON 2

Learning Goal: Students will be able to plan the beginning, middle, and end of their writing, as well as key details for each section.

I DO: Go back to your three-column organizer and review the beginning, middle, and end. Invite students to let you know what they might be wondering about in each section. This helps the writer know what the reader is interested in. Add two or three (or more) relevant details to each section.

WE DO: Revisit the trifold planner that the group collaborated on during the previous lesson. Invite students to suggest relevant details and add them to each section.

YOU DO: Have students revisit their own planners to add several details to each section. You might want to give them an opportunity to meet with a writing partner to share their B-M-E summaries and have the partners ask each other questions about each section, either before or after the writer adds details.

> Some students need parameters for writing, especially struggling students. You might want to start out by specifying a *minimum* number of details for each section, such as 3-5-3.

MINILESSON 3

Learning Goal: Students will be able to plan an opening and closing for their piece of writing.

I DO: Go back to one of your three-column organizer examples and fold the paper (or draw a line) to create a row about 1 inch wide across the top and the bottom. Think aloud as you consider what might be a "grabber" opening and write it in the top row. Do the same with a "bow-on-the-present" ending at the bottom.

WE DO: Go through the same process as a shared writing experience with a collaborative topic.

YOU DO: Have students revisit their own planners to create a row across the top and bottom to craft an interesting opening and closing for their piece.

Trifold Planner

Opening		
Beginning	**Middle**	**End**
Closing		

Pembroke Publishers© 2018 *Marvelous Minilessons for Teaching Intermediate Writing, Grades 3–8* by Lori Jamison Rog ISBN 978-1-55138-329-3

Listing or Layering

Learning Goal: Students will be able to distinguish the difference between listing a string of events and layering by elaborating on key details.

I DO: Display and read together "My Trip to Disneyland" below. It's pretty easy to see that this piece is just a list of all the things they did at Disneyland. Compare it to "My Memory" at the opening of this chapter (page 85) which elaborates on one special experience at Disneyland. That's the difference between listing and layering. A writer's term for layering is *elaboration*; in other words, it's adding details to details.

My Trip to Disneyland

I went to Disneyland with my brother, grandparents, and cousins. We checked into our hotel and the next day we went on all the rides. They had a light parade and we watched it at night. My favorite ride was Star Tours. We also went on the Pirates of the Caribbean and Haunted Mansion. I liked Splash Mountain too. The next morning we went to Knots Berry Farm. We went swimming in a large pool. We went home the very next day.

WE DO: Ask the students to talk to their writing partners about the techniques the writer of "My Memory" has used to add layers of information to her topic. For example, she:

- described what she did on the ride
- included her feelings and emotions
- used descriptive language such as "whooshing" and "frogs jumping in my stomach"

Provide students with a short guided writing exercise to complete in pairs or small groups. Reproduce "Fun Foods at the Fair" (page 92) and have students choose one or two details to add layers of elaboration. (You can find an example below.) You will notice that the layers are written in italics.

One of my favorite things to do at the summer fair is eat! I could eat all day, starting with mini donuts in the morning, followed by a midmorning snack of a candied apple or a chocolate-covered banana. For lunch, I like to eat a big slice of pizza *dripping with cheese* and ice cream on a stick. *My mouth starts to water at the mere thought of the creamy and crunchy tastes of vanilla ice cream dipped in chocolate coating and rolled in peanuts. It's a little taste of heaven right here on the fairgrounds.*

YOU DO: Ask students to revisit one of their existing drafts to revise by adding a layer of information to any key detail.

Fun Foods at the Fair

One of my favorite things to do at the summer fair is eat! I could eat all day, starting with mini donuts in the morning, followed by a midmorning snack of a candied apple or a chocolate-covered banana. For lunch, I like to eat a big slice of pizza and ice cream on a stick. By afternoon, I'm ready for a corn dog and I always leave room for a final feast of a sugary funnel cake.

Don't Tell Me, Show Me!

"Show, Don't Tell" has been described as the "golden rule of writing." The bonus of this minilesson is that it not only teaches an important writing strategy, it incorporates a grammar lesson as well, teaching students to use vivid verbs in their "show me" statements.

Literature Link: *The Dirty Cowboy* by Amy Timberlake is a picture book with an engaging story, delightful illustrations, and many literary devices, including terrific examples of showing rather than telling.

Learning Goal: Students will be able to create interesting "showing" details to supplement or replace "telling" statements in their writing.

I DO: Read (and display, if possible) the first four pages of *The Dirty Cowboy*. Ask students how they know the cowboy is dirty when the author has never even used that word. Showing instead of telling is one of the most powerful tricks that authors use.

WE DO: Create a visual of this concept using a "five-finger planner" (Reproduce a hand shape or simply trace your hand so it is visible to all the students.) On the "palm" of the hand shape, write the telling statement, "The cowboy was dirty." Have students contribute showing details from the text and write them on the fingers of the hand shape.

Point out to the students that the telling statements usually have verbs of being (*is, was, were, are, am*) while showing statements tend to have more vivid verbs (see page 105). Highlight the verbs in Timberlake's "showing" details on the five-finger planner.

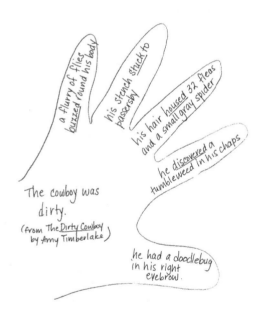

Choose a statement like "The house was haunted." Display an enlarged five-finger planner and write this telling statement on the palm. Invite the students to contribute showing details that support the telling statement. Encourage the use of vivid verbs.

For additional practice, have the students work in pairs or small groups to choose a "telling" statement and generate rich "showing" details on a five-finger planner.

YOU DO: Instruct students to go back into a piece of their own writing and highlight a telling statement. Have them revise by replacing or adding to the telling statement with one or more showing details.

Telling Statements

- My bedroom is really a mess.

- That person is extremely rich.

- I think the house was haunted.

- My brother was furious.

- My pet is so funny.

- He/She is a really good friend.

- My brother/sister is a walking disaster.

- It was a terrible storm.

- It is the most beautiful place in the world.

Add an Anecdote

Learning Goal: Students will be able to write anecdotes or examples to elaborate on ideas in their writing.

I DO: An anecdote is a little story that elaborates or gives an example. An anecdote could be funny or sad or surprising. Writers add anecdotes to prove a point, support an idea, or add voice and interest to a piece of writing. Talk about the example in this excerpt from *Ghost House* by Paul Kropp:

> *We were together in preschool, friends in grade two and best buddies since grade six... If there is a problem, then all of us have to fix it. Like the time Hammy's line drive smashed Mrs. Headly's window. We all chipped in on that one. After all, it was my baseball, A.J.'s bat and Zach's pitch that got the ball going. We are that tight.*

WE DO: Compare this excerpt with the example "My Friends" below, written by a Grade Six student. You might make the observation that this piece just offers a list of ideas about friends. It would be more interesting with some examples or anecdotes that provide layers of information about the friends. Draw students' attention to a statement like, "they're there when I need them." Have them collaborate with a partner to invent a short anecdote to add to this statement. You might use an interactive writing approach to enlarge and revise the "My Friends" piece or simply leave this as an oral exercise.

My Friends

My friends are EXTREMELY cool because they are my friends. My friends are not ordinary, they're the opposite of ordinary because they're there when I need them. They keep me from doing stuff I might regret later in life. Friends are friendly people you should be able to keep secrets with. Friends make me laugh and keep me from getting bored. Friends are people you can trust, who won't hurt you or take your things. Friends make you laugh when you're down and feeling blue. Friends can tell when you're sad so you can't hide your feelings from your friends. Friends make you smile no matter if it's snowing, raining, or other bad storms. They always make you have a smile. Friends are caring. When you get hurt, they're always there. Helpful, kind, and caring—that's my friends.

YOU DO: Have students practice adding an anecdote to a piece of their own writing.

Slo-Mo Writing

It may be hard to believe, but slowing down the most interesting part of a story can actually make it more exciting. Slo-Mo Writing is a writer's technique that involves describing an event as if it were happening in slow motion. Slowing the action down builds suspense and lets the reader savour the most exciting part of the story.

Learning Goal: Students will be able to elaborate on a detail in their writing by describing a moment of action in slow motion.

I DO: Display these two versions of throwing a snowball.

Mallory threw a snowball at her dad as he came around the corner.	With a sneaky smile, Mallory reached for a handful of soft sticky snow. She carefully molded the ball so that it fit just right in her hand. At just the right moment, she reached back, aimed, and hurled the snowball forward with all her might. Flying through the air, it almost seemed to stop in midair before hitting its target: right between her dad's shoulder blades!

The time elapsed between picking up the handful of snow and the snowball hitting Mallory's dad was less than a minute, but in the second example, the author has taken four long sentences to describe it. It's like the event was happening in slow motion. Authors often use this technique, because *slowing down* the writing actually *speeds up* the suspense and action. We can use Slo-Mo writing to describe more than just actions; it gives the writer opportunities to describe the character's thoughts, feelings, and even facial expression. Slo-Mo writing sends a signal to readers that this is an important part of the writing.

Slo-Mo Writing Practice Prompts:
• Falling off a ladder • Diving into a pool or lake • Eating a loaded hot dog • Scoring a goal • Crossing the finish line

WE DO: Have students work in pairs or small groups to select one of the practice prompts (or a topic of their own) to describe in slow motion. They should use at least four sentences to describe a single moment in time.

YOU DO: Have students revisit their own previous drafts to find a place where they can expand an exciting event with Slo-Mo writing.

Dabble in Dialogue

Used judiciously and purposefully, dialogue can define characters, provide background information, and add voice and interest to the writing. Too much dialogue makes the writing sound like a Seinfeld script—talking about nothing! We want our intermediate students to be able to write interesting and engaging dialogue that enhances the overall text. We also want them to be able to conquer the accompanying conventions: setting off speech with quotation marks, separating a tag line and the talk with punctuation, and starting a new paragraph with each new speaker. It is an ideal opportunity to teach conventions in the context of authentic writing.

Learning Goal: Students will be able to inject dialogue effectively into a piece of writing, using quotation marks and tag lines.

I DO: When there are two or more characters in a story, the author usually has them talk to each other. We call this dialogue—a conversation among two or more characters in written text. Dialogue rarely tells a whole story, but it is most effective when inserted into a story here and there. Too much dialogue can make a piece of writing boring. But little bits of carefully chosen dialogue make the writing more interesting and energetic. The excerpt from *Winner* by Paul Kropp below shows how a writer can use a small bit of dialogue to add extra information and more voice to the narrative. The narrator could have just said, "My mom had won the lottery." But this dialogue conveys both the mom's excitement and the narrator's concern—and sets the reader up to wonder (just as Josh did) how this could possibly be anything but good news.

> *Inside our room, my mom let out a scream. It was something I'd never heard before — a scream of joy.*
>
> *"I won!" my mom screamed again. "I won! I won!"*
>
> *"Josh, I think I've got a problem here," I told my friend.*
>
> *"It sounds like good news to me," he said.*
>
> *My mom came rushing out the door. She was holding a lottery ticket in her hand.*

Take advantage of the opportunity to point out the way that quotation marks frame the speech. The part that tells who was talking (*my mom screamed*) is called the "tag line."

WE DO: Use a shared or interactive writing approach with the whole group or have students work in pairs to inject at least three lines of dialogue into a sample piece of text. The reproducible on page 99 is a doctored version of another sample from *Winner*. (The actual text is shown on page 98.)

YOU DO: Invite students to revise one of their previous drafts or a work in progress by inserting short bits of dialogue.

ACTUAL TEXT FROM **WINNER**:

Mom promised to be quiet. And I didn't tell a soul. We had to make a plan for the money.

But when I got to school the next day, the news was all over.

"Hey, it's Ryan the rich kid," shouted the first guy I saw.

"Ryan, whatcha gonna buy?" shouted another kid. "A new car? A BMW? A Porsche?"

"Ryan," whispered a girl named Tracy. "I always thought you were a geek. But now—well I can see how cool you really are. You want to come over to my house?"

How did they all find out? I only had to think for a second. Then the answer was clear. Josh.

"You told," I said.

"I had to," Josh admitted. I called a couple of people. And then...it got out of hand." He looked kind of embarrassed. "You didn't say it was a secret."

Add Some Dialogue

Mom promised to be quiet. And I didn't tell a soul. We had to make a plan for the money.

But when I got to school the next day, the news was all over. The first kid I saw called me a rich kid. Another kid asked me what I was going to buy. A girl named Tracey told me she used to think I was a geek but now she realized how cool I was. Even the teachers had found out.

How did they all find out? I only had to think for a second. Then the answer was clear. Josh. He just told a couple of people but then it got out of hand. He said I never told him it was a secret.

Adapted from *Winner* by Paul Kropp

Pembroke Publishers © 2018 *Marvelous Minilessons for Teaching Intermediate Writing, Grades 3–8* by Lori Jamison Rog ISBN 978-1-55138-329-3

"Stars and Wishes" Peer Conferences

Many developing writers have trouble seeing their writing from someone else's point of view. Peer conferences help writers find out what details might be missing or confusing to a reader. And giving meaningful feedback to another writer gives the peer a deeper understanding of writer's techniques.

Learning Goal: Students will be able to identify strengths (stars) and areas that require more elaboration (wishes) in a peer's writing.

I DO: Talk to the students about the difficulty of seeing your own writing from the point of view of a reader. Sometimes a writer needs to talk to another person in order to know what details might be confusing or missing or out of place. These conversations with another student are called *peer conferences*.

A good conference has two parts: the "stars" (compliments) and the "wishes" (questions or suggestions). The writer reads his piece aloud; the peer doesn't look at the writing. In this way, the peer is able to focus on the ideas of the piece rather than the conventions.

The peer always starts a peer conference with something he or she enjoyed or found interesting or that the writer has done well. Be specific! For example, "That detail about your cat drinking coffee was very funny" is a much more useful comment for a writer than "I liked it."

The "wish" is usually something you'd like to know more about or you don't understand. We use statements like: *I wish you would tell more about…* or *I wish you would explain….* Students have to learn that this is not a criticism of the piece and they need to be careful about the writer's feelings. The "wishes" do not evaluate the quality of the writing, but focus on making the writing more clear and effective.

WE DO: Use a sample piece such as "People and Paper Clips Don't Mix" (below) and ask students to suggest Stars and Wishes. Some suggestions may be found in the box on the left. Two questions are enough for this piece of writing. It is now time for the writer to take the suggestions they have been given and decide what information they want to add to their piece so that it is clearer to a reader.

YOU DO: Assign partners and have them discuss with each other, then establish this as a routine part of the Publication Journey (page 26).

Stars & Wishes for "People and Paper Clips"

STARS:
- good descriptions like "puny little mouth"
- opening hooks the reader
- ending is funny

WISHES:
- I wish you would explain why the two little kids were playing while everyone else was asleep.
- I wonder how the uncle knew they were in trouble.

People and Paper Clips Don't Mix

Once I did something that I'll never do again. My cousin and I were playing in my brother's room. We were just toddlers at the time. Everyone else was sleeping. I found a paper clip and I put it in my mouth. I swallowed it and it got stuck in my throat. I started to choke out blood. My mom and my brother woke up. My uncle ran to the room and stuck his fingers into my puny little mouth. He felt it, got a grip on it and pulled it out. Then we all went to the hospital to see if there were any more paper clips in my mouth. But there weren't any more. My uncle actually saved my life. And do you know what? My dad slept through the whole thing!

Chapter 7   The Writer's Craft: Writing With Rhythm And Flair

Maui Dreams

I watch the morning sun
set the sky on fire
over the mountain.
I bask on the beach,
soaking up the sun.
I splash in the salty surf.
I scan the horizon
for the silhouettes of breaching whales
and diving dolphins.
Black sand tickles my toes
as I stroll along the beach.
Windsurfers' neon sails
skim across the shimmering sea.
I watch the sun
drop below the horizon
leaving the island in darkness.
The alarm clock rings.
It's back to reality.
Forty below in Saskatchewan.

The previous chapter of this book dealt with helping students develop the content of writing: choosing a topic, making a plan, and elaborating on ideas. This chapter examines the craft of writing—not so much *what* the writer says but *how* the writer says it.

The poem at the beginning of this chapter was written by a Grade Six student. She has handpicked every word: the vivid verbs, the rhythmical phrases, the varied sentences, and the surprise ending. Here is a young writer who knows something about craft.

Craft has been variously defined as style, polish, and eloquence. This chapter will focus on the way writers choose and use words to give their writing fluency and flair. We want them to vary sentences, experiment with sound, and search for the "just right" rather than the "all right" combination of words.

Perhaps the most important element of *craft* is the writer's "voice." Whether defined as *tone, mood,* or *style,* voice is that hard-to-define aspect of writing that speaks to a reader. It reflects the way that a writer would like the reader to respond to the writing—to laugh or cry; to be angry or sympathetic; entertained, or amazed. Certainly voice is generated by the writer's passion for the topic, but it's also shown in the words the writer has chosen and the way the writer has put those words together.

> *Vocabulary instruction should be woven into all parts of the curriculum. But how do we get students to use these interesting and powerful words? One of my favorite tricks is "The Gift of a Word." When learning new vocabulary in a piece of literature or non-fiction, invite students to select two or three words they might use in their own writing and record them on sticky notes. They should keep the sticky notes in their writing folders until they've used the words, then pass them on as a "gift" to someone else.*

When it comes to choosing words, many students tend to think that bigger is better. In reality, however, the best word isn't necessarily the fanciest word. Young writers need to learn to use resources for word choice without developing "thesaurusitis," that dreaded syndrome of synonymous words that don't necessarily fit the context of the writing. Let's face it, pretentious verbiage is often repellant to the peruser of print; in other words, too many fancy words can send a reader running for the hills!

Of course, good writing is more than just individual words. Writers must group those words in special structures called sentences. Why are so many students confused about sentences? Maybe it's because someone has told them that a sentence is a complete thought. That has to be one of the most misleading things we teachers tell students! We have plenty of complete thoughts that aren't complete sentences. ("Oh, no!" "Not again!" "Guilty as charged.") And, let's face it, there are many grammatically correct sentences that, taken out of context, are pretty incomplete to a reader or listener; consider: "The llama smeared lipstick on her eyes and applied mascara to her toenails." There's nothing wrong with this sentence grammatically, but there's nothing about it that makes sense. A "complete thought" is more about context and a "sentence" is more about grammatical structure. A sentence is, essentially, a special group of words that must have a subject (who or what) and a predicate (is or does). Once students have that foundational understanding, they can create, build, embellish, and flip sentences to their hearts' content.

Varying sentence length and structure can add fluency and rhythm, as well as interest and shape to the piece of writing as a whole. There are four main ways that writers can vary sentences: by using different sentence types, by varying sentence structures, by changing sentence beginnings, and by varying the lengths of sentences.

As a rule, writers tend to use long, flowing sentences for description and short, quick sentences for action. Too many sentences of the same length and structure can sound choppy and monotonous, not unlike driving in stop-and-start traffic.

But if all the sentences are too long, the writing can become unwieldy, and readers may get lost on the way. The solution is variety. The occasional **Very Short Sentence (VSS)**—or sentence fragment—of three-to-five words can punch up a series of longer flowing sentences and make the reader sit up and take notice.

Allowing students to use sentence fragments in writing is controversial among teachers. For the most part, we want our students to understand and use complete sentences, particularly in formal writing. Sometimes, however, a fragment can be powerful enough to stand alone and add punch to the text. Why should we prohibit our students from using a structure that they see in published writing all the time? And that includes sentences beginning with conjunctions like *and* and *but,* which occur in almost 10% of published writing, according to the Chicago Manual of Style!

Teaching students to craft their ideas effectively is one of the most rewarding parts of the Writing Workshop. Using interesting words, clever comparisons, figurative language, and varied sentences in writing is sort of like pinning a diamond brooch to an elegant gown: it adds a little *bling*.

MINILESSONS IN THIS CHAPTER:

Minilesson Name	Page	Learning Focus
TAP into Voice	104	Considering topic, audience, and purpose
Vivid Verbs	105	Energizing writing with strong verbs
The Magic of Three	107	Grouping words and phrases in threes
Say it with a Simile	109	Using interesting comparisons
What Does Red Sound Like?	111	Crafting sensory images
Pop in a Popper	113	Adding appositive phrases to modify nouns
The VSS	115	Using very short sentences and fragments
Flip the Sentence	116	Chunking and reorganizing sentences for variety

TAP into Voice

It's often said that "voice" is the fingerprint of the writer on the page. In truth, voice is as much about the reader as the writer. Good writers use their voice to generate an emotional response from their readers, whether it be laughter, anger, or sadness. That's why audience and purpose are just as important considerations as the topic when writing.

Learning Goal: Students will be able to consider topic, audience and purpose as they compose their writing.

I DO: Show students a few short pieces of writing, such as those below and invite them to speculate about whom each one is written for and why the writer wrote the piece. Talk about how each piece of writing might be different if the audience or purpose was different. Introduce the acronym TAP—Topic, Audience (or reader), and Purpose (or reason for writing). A list of different purposes for writing is provided at the end of this lesson.

---

1. I am writing to request a copy of the free magazine you advertised on your website. It will be helpful for my school report. Please send it to the address below.
2. Hooray! It's my birthday party! Please come Tuesday at 4:00!
3. Once upon a time, there were three bears: a mommy bear, a daddy bear, and a baby bear, just like you.
4. Thanks for the great present! You always know just what I want. Love you lots!

WE DO: Provide students with the Guided Writing activity about chocolate cake to write individually. I like to assign one of the four prompts to each student, then have them share their writing with teams to reflect on how different audiences affect the voice and tone of a piece of writing, even a piece that is about the same topic.

YOU DO: Begin to establish a writing workshop routine asking students to consider their TAP — Topic, Audience and Purpose—as they prepare to write any piece.

	Topic	Audience	Purpose
1		Weight Watchers meeting	Bragging about how you resisted temptation
2	Description of a piece of chocolate cake	Young children	Lecturing on why it's bad for you
3		Waiter	Persuading diners to order it
4		Diner	Complaining about how bad it tasted

Vivid Verbs

Of all the parts of speech, verbs do the most to invigorate writing. Insipid verbs, such as went, said, *or* took, *usually require an adverb to let the reader know just how that verb was carried out. But when a writer uses a more vivid and precise verb, such as* stroll, murmur, *or* devour, *the reader gets a clear picture of the action without a modifier.*

Learning Goal: Students will be able to identify and use vigorous verbs in their writing.

I DO: Review with the students what a verb is and what function it serves in a sentence. Verbs convey an action (as in *run* or *talk*) or a state of being (like *is* and *were*). Every sentence must have a verb, and, as a rule, the stronger the verbs, the livelier the writing is. A great text for vivid verbs is Jack Prelutsky's poem "The Turkey Shot out of the Oven." Display a copy of the poem and read it together, inviting students to take note of verbs that are particularly vivid or memorable to them.

WE DO: Now that the students can identify vivid verbs in a passage, have them practice revising a text for verb choice. The reproducible text on the following page is an excerpt from the novel *The Countess and Me* (2002) by Paul Kropp, with the actual verbs removed and replaced by more mundane words. Have students work in pairs to revise the piece by substituting more energetic verbs. After completing the task, the students might be interested in comparing their words with the author's original text (found at the end of this lesson). Reinforce that this is not an exercise in right and wrong or trying to match the author's words; students may actually prefer some of their own word choices. In writing, most words are open to debate!

YOU DO: Have students revise a piece of their own writing by replacing at least two dull verbs with more vivid verbs. Older students might also be asked to identify any adverbs in their writing and consider whether to delete them and use a stronger verb.

> A great poem for reinforcing energetic verbs is "The Turkey Shot out of the Oven" by Jack Prelutsky. The rollicking rhythm and surprise ending are sure to engage your students, not to mention the wonderful word choice like *"The turkey shot out of the oven and rocketed into the air, It knocked every plate off the table and partly demolished a chair"* (verse 1).

ACTUAL TEXT FROM **THE COUNTESS AND ME***:*

I wasn't in my right mind when I stormed out of the house. I was so crazy mad that I didn't have a plan or strategy. It was Mordock's idea—break in, steal something and terrorize an old lady.

I scribbled some lame excuse to my mother, then took off for Cullen's house. I dashed over to the east side, snuck along the back and tried the patio door. Locked. To one side was a basement window, half-open already. I took my house key and sliced the screen, then pushed the screen up and slid out the window. Easy as pie.

Add Vivid Verbs

I wasn't in my right mind when I <u>went</u> out of the house. I was so crazy mad that I didn't have a plan or strategy. It was Mordock's idea—break in, steal something and <u>scare</u> an old lady.

I <u>wrote</u> some lame excuse to my mother, then took off for Cullen's house. I <u>walked</u> over to the east side, <u>went</u> along the back and tried the patio door. Locked. To one side was a basement window, half-open already. I took my house key and <u>cut</u> the screen, then pushed the screen up and slid out the window. <u>Easy as pie</u>.

Adapted from *The Countess and Me*, by Paul Kropp

Pembroke Publishers © 2018 *Marvelous Minilessons for Teaching Intermediate Writing, Grades 3–8* by Lori Jamison Rog ISBN 978-1-55138-329-3

The Magic of Three

"I came, I saw, I conquered," said Julius Caesar (at least according to William Shake-speare). There is something magical about putting ideas together in threes. Linguists call it a "tricolon;" we call it "the magic of three." Tricolons are easy to read, easy to say, and easy to remember. (See what I mean?) Great orators know that tricolons pack a persuasive punch. They also add rhythm and cadence to the sound of the writing.

Learning Goal: Students will be able to put words, phrases, and sentences in groups of three to make their writing flow more rhythmically.

I DO: There's something about our English language that lends itself to putting words and phrases and even sentences in groups of three. Somehow, putting words or groups of words in threes not only makes them sound more musical, it also makes them more memorable to a reader. Share the famous examples below with students.

Famous Examples of The Magic of Three

- "Tell me and I forget. Teach me and I remember. Involve me and I learn." (B. Franklin)
- "Life, liberty, and the pursuit of happiness." (US Declaration of Independence)
- "Peace, order, and good government." (Canadian Constitution Act)
- "Liberté, égalité, fraternité." (motto of the French Revolution)
- "A happy life is one spent in learning, earning, and yearning." (unknown)
- "Government of the people, by the people, for the people." (Abraham Lincoln)

WE DO: Here's a great opportunity to teach grammar in context. Draw students' attention to the fact that the words or groups of words in each of the famous tricolons have the same grammatical structure: three nouns, three verb phrases, three sentences, etc. Together, construct a set of rules for the magic of three:

- They all must convey a common idea.
- They all must have the same structure.
- Words and phrases need commas between them. (Sentences need periods, of course.)
- They must sound rhythmical to the ear.

Provide guided practice for your students in pairs or small groups. Have them complete the reproducible on page 108.

YOU DO: Ask students to look for examples of The Magic of Three in an existing piece of their own writing. Writers often use this technique without even being aware of it! Suggest that they incorporate The Magic of Three into a piece of writing, either in a rough draft or during revision.

The Magic of Three

Complete the following sentences with parallel words or phrases.

(Three nouns) _____, _____, and _____ swam by us in the Aquarium.

(Three verbs) I was _____, _____, and _____ on the trampoline.

(Three parallel phrases) At school, it's important to _____, _____, and _____.

Pembroke Publishers © 2018 *Marvelous Minilessons for Teaching Intermediate Writing, Grades 3–8* by Lori Jamison Rog ISBN 978-1-55138-329-3

Say It With a Simile

What's "as varied as snowflakes, as handy as tacks, as thrilling as danger, unlikely as yaks?" The simile, according to Norton Juster, in his book As: A Surfeit of Similes. *Grammatically speaking, a simile draws a comparison between two ideas using the words* like *or* as. *Fresh and original similes make writing more interesting and help readers perceive ideas in new ways. This lesson uses a Carousel Brainstorming routine that can be used in many different contexts.*

Learning Goal: Students will be able to identify and use fresh and original similes to make their writing more interesting and engaging.

> **Literature Link:** This minilesson uses examples from *As: A Surfeit of Similes* by Norton Juster (1989), a lively read-aloud packed with similes in rhyming text.

I DO: Provide students with a list of common similes or use some examples from *As: A Surfeit of Similes*, such as "As fair as a lily, as empty as air, as fresh as a daisy, as cross as a bear" or, "As flat as a pancake, as warm as your socks, as short as bad tempers, as constant as clocks."

Ask students to talk to their partners about what these phrases have in common: each one provides a comparison using the structure *as…as.* (Of course, similes can also use the word *like,* as in describing something so difficult that it was "like putting toothpaste back in the tube.")

The literary term for this kind of phrase is *simile.* (Here's a spelling mnemonic that's also a simile: *simile* is like *smile* with an extra *i.*) Writers use similes to help readers understand or view an idea in a new way by associating it with something familiar.

WE DO: Discuss some of the similes above and invite students to suggest some similes that they know. Compare similes that are fresh and original with similes have been used so much that they're a little tired, such as "dark as night" or "shines like silver." Take an example like "as empty as air" and brainstorm some other comparisons to describe "as empty as_____."

Use a "carousel" approach to give students practice in generating interesting similes. Prepare 6-8 pieces of chart paper by writing a different simile stem (like the examples below) at the top of each page.

Post the charts around the room, at an accessible height for students to write on them.

Divide the students into groups of three or four and place each group at a different chart. Assign one person in each group to be the writer; the rest will be the brainstormers. Time the students for two to three minutes. During that time, the groups will brainstorm as many words and phrases as they can to complete the simile on their chart. When the time is up, each group cycles to the next chart in "carousel" fashion, with two or three minutes to add to what the previous group has written on the chart. Continue until each group has visited three or four charts. (Monitor the students; when they seem to be out of ideas, signal a movement to the next chart. The timing will become shorter as students move through the carousel.)

When each group has had an opportunity to contribute to at least three or four charts, make one last carousel. Have the groups look at a chart they have not contributed to and discuss which they think are the most effective similes on the chart. Invite each group to read the three most creative similes on the chart in front of them. Talk with the students about what makes one simile more effective than another—fresh original ideas, clear comparisons that make sense, vivid images with strong word choice.

The great advantage to the Brainstorming Carousel is that it gets the students up and moving. However, an alternative technique is "brainwriting", where the students stay in place and the paper cycles from one group to the next.

Simile Stems

- as soft as
- as bright as
- as strong as

- as loud as
- as dirty as
- as sparkly as

- as tiny as
- as scratchy as

YOU DO: Have students revise a piece of writing in their writing folders to insert at least one simile.

What Does Red Sound Like? Using Sensory Images

When we think about descriptive writing, we usually think of visual images. But descriptions of smells, tastes, sounds, and textures can also be unique and effective ways to elaborate on an idea in writing. This lesson invites students to practice using sensory details to describe ordinary concepts such as colors. You might choose to use the Brainstorming Carousel routine from the Similes lesson (page 109).

Learning Goal: Students will be able to elaborate on a key idea or detail with sensory images.

I DO: Tell students that showing rather than telling isn't just about creating visual pictures; writers often use other sensory images as well. It's pretty easy to convey the smells and tastes of a Thanksgiving dinner or the texture of a sandy beach under your feet. But clever writers can also associate sensory images with unusual things like colors.

Display and read excerpts from the book *Hailstones and Halibut Bones* to convey some of the smells, sounds, tastes, and textures the author has related to colors. Pause frequently to talk about unique images that Mary O'Neill has used, such as, "White is the beautiful broken lace of snowflakes falling on your face" (p. 29).

WE DO: As a shared writing exercise, choose a color and invite the students to brainstorm as many sensory images as they can. You can start with a basic color such as purple, or choose a more exotic paint chip color from your local paint store. The Senses Chart below was a collaborative effort of from a fifth-grade class based on a paint chip color called "Caribbean Coral." Then have students choose a color (or choose a paint chip) to work in pairs to complete the chart on page 112.

> **Literature Link:** The classic *Hailstones and Halibut Bones* (1990) by Mary O'Neill is full of wonderful sensory images about colors—all conveyed in rhyming text.

> Add a twist to this lesson by gathering a collection of paint chips from your local paint store. Have students draw a chip at random and create sensory images related to its appearance and name.

Color	Looks Like	Sounds Like	Smells Like	Tastes Like	Feels Like
Caribbean Coral	- weathered brick on an old house - a bright pinky orange sunset on a clear night.	- Calypso music with maracas and drums.	- wet sandy beaches - smoldering embers as a fire is dying down	- cantaloupe juice dripping down your chin	- rough stone with bumpy, pointy parts, like coral - warmer than pink but cooler than red

YOU DO: Suggest that students look for a detail in an existing piece of writing that they can elaborate on by adding an unusual sensory image.

The Senses Chart

Color	Looks Like	Sounds Like	Smells Like	Tastes Like	Feels Like

Pembroke Publishers © 2018 *Marvelous Minilessons for Teaching Intermediate Writing, Grades 3–8* by Lori Jamison Rog ISBN 978-1-55138-329-3

Pop in a Popper

This lesson introduces the appositive, a group of words that we "pop" into a sentence to define or explain a noun. (There, I just did it: I added a group of words to define the word appositive.) Unlike an adjective, which goes before a noun in English, an appositive is usually (but not always) popped in after the noun. A popper is embedded in a sentence, separated from the core subject and predicate by commas (or sometimes dashes). The sentence remains intact, whether we pop in or pop out the popper.

Learning Goal: Students will be able to embed descriptive phrases, or poppers, into sentences, with appropriate punctuation, in order to elaborate on nouns.

I DO: Link this lesson to students' prior knowledge about elaborating on nouns using adjectives. Another way to modify a noun is by inserting a descriptive phrase after the noun, in the middle or at the end of the sentence. We call them "poppers" because we "pop" them into a sentence that is quite complete without them. In Below are some examples from young adult literature. Invite students to identify the noun and the popper in each sentence.

Examples of Appositives from Literature

- *Gilly gave little William Ernest the most fearful face in all her collection of scary looks, <u>a cross between Count Dracula and Godzilla.</u>* (Katherine Paterson, *The Great Gilly Hopkins*)
- *I took the pearls out of my pocket, <u>the three milky spheres the Nereid had given me in Santa Monica.</u>* (Rick Riordan, *The Lightning Thief*).
- *And then I saw the black car, <u>a weathered Ford,</u> parked in Charlie's driveway—and heard Edward mutter something unintelligible in a low, harsh voice.* (Stephenie Meyer, *Twilight*).
- *Filch owned a cat called Mrs. Norris, <u>a scrawny, dust-colored creature with bulging, lamp-like eyes just like Filch's.</u>* (J.K. Rowling, *Harry Potter and the Sorcerer's Stone*).

Note the punctuation: usually the popper is separated from the rest of the sentence with commas, though occasionally a writer will use dashes instead. Also, the popper might include the words, "who is" or "which was" but usually those words are implied.

WE DO: Use a shared or interactive writing approach to add appositives to the following sentences.

- My brother, _____, goes to games with his face painted in his team's colors.
- Scrabble, _____, is enjoyed by players of all ages.

If you feel the students still need additional practice before independent application, reproduce the sentences on page 114 for students to use to pop in poppers.

YOU DO: Have students revise a piece of writing in their writing folders by popping in at least one popper phrase.

Pop in a Popper!

Add a popper to each of these sentences.

- Wayne Gretzky once scored five goals in one game!

- The kangaroo is native to Australia.

- Mr. Smith repaired our broken water pipe.

- J.K. Rowling wrote the *Harry Potter* series.

- I got these boots at Southland Mall.

Pembroke Publishers © 2018 *Marvelous Minilessons for Teaching Intermediate Writing, Grades 3–8* by Lori Jamison Rog ISBN 978-1-55138-329-3

The VSS (Very Short Sentence)

Learning Goal: Students will be able to use short sentences and sentence fragments to effectively add tone and fluency to their writing.

I DO: We've spent a lot of time over the years reinforcing that a complete sentence needs a subject (who or what) and a predicate (verb). But sometimes writers will deliberately use a group of words that don't have both of these conditions. That's why we call them sentence fragments. Revisit the following excerpt from *The Countess and Me* by Paul Kropp. Point out to the students that in the second paragraph there are two Very Short Sentences (VSS). In fact, they aren't really complete sentences at all, but sentence fragments or incomplete sentences. Notice in this example, that both times the writer balanced long, flowing, "magic-of-three" sentences with punchy VSS (Very Short Sentences).

Excerpt from *The Countess and Me* by Paul Kropp

I wasn't in my right mind when I stormed out of the house. I was so crazy mad that I didn't have a plan or strategy. It was Mordock's idea—break in, steal something and terrorize an old lady.

I scribbled some lame excuse to my mother, then took off for Cullen's house. I dashed over to the east side, snuck along the back and tried the patio door. Locked. To one side was a basement window, half-open already. I took my house key and sliced the screen, then pushed the screen up and slid out the window. Easy as pie.

If there are too many short sentences, a piece of writing can sound choppy. But the occasional short (three-to-five word) sentence or sentence fragment can add some punch to a piece of writing. Exclamations, such as "What a game!" are commonly used as Very Short Sentences. Sometimes they are complete sentences ("It was mine.") and sometimes they're not ("Mine. All mine."). Their purpose is always to add energy to a piece of writing and make it flow in a more rhythmical way.

WE DO: Use a shared writing approach with the whole group or have students work in small groups to revise this piece of writing and insert or substitute at least two Very Short Sentences (or Fragments).

The Day I Spent in the Year 3333

When I woke up, my bed felt surprisingly springy and my pillow seemed to be a cloud. I crawled out of bed and stood on the floor, examining my room. Suddenly a recliner came up behind me and forced me to sit on it by running into the back of my knees. The recliner took me to a long room that resembled a touchless car wash. I was utterly surprised when water, soap and shampoo sprayed on me. I was almost knocked backwards as a large gust of warm air blew at me. Then it was all over and I walked to two giant doors. I opened the doors to find a large room full of clothes.

YOU DO: Invite students to examine an existing draft to find a place where they might insert a VSS or fragment for effect.

Flip the Sentence

Just as too many sentences of the same length can make writing tedious to read, too many sentences of the same structure can be monotonous as well. Even changing the first few words can make a difference to sentence fluency, One writer's trick for varying sentences is to change the order of the words: flip a prepositional phrase from the end of the sentence to the beginning, or flip two clauses. In this lesson, students learn to identify sentence chunks (prepositional phrases and subordinate clauses) and experiment with flipping their order. This is also an opportunity to teach students about using commas to separate a phrase or clause from the rest of the sentence.

Learning Goal: Students will be able to change the order of words in a sentence correctly and effectively in order to vary the sentence structure.

I DO: Display a pair of sentences, such as:

- There was a mysterious gift in the middle of the room.
- In the middle of the room, there was a mysterious gift.

Point out that the two sentences are both grammatically correct and say exactly the same thing, but the two parts of the sentence are "flipped around." When there is a group of words that tells *where* (like "in the middle of the room") or *when* (like "after dinner"), you can flip that group of words to different places in the sentence.

WE DO: Use the following excerpt from *The Secret Knowledge of Grown-ups*, or choose one of your own.

> Just like carrot seeds become carrots and bean seeds become beans, fingernail scraps become fingers. After growing under your bed or between the sofa pillows for about three months, the new fingers leave their nests and go crawling around the house.
>
> At first, this isn't too much of a problem. With their dimpled knuckles and sunny dispositions, the baby fingers are actually kind of cute. As they get older, the fingers start behaving badly.

With the students, analyze these five sentences. First, divide each sentence into chunks by separating the *where, when,* or *how* (prepositional) phrases from the kernel of the sentence. Invite students to note the purpose of phrases like "at first" or "after growing under your bed" or "just like"; they tell when, where, or how. We call them "prepositional phrases" because they start with prepositions.

Look at the sentence: "The fingers start behaving badly as they get older." Ask the students how it might be "flipped." There might be different ways to correctly flip a sentence, but some variations will sound better than others. Trust your ear!

The reproducible on page 118, contains a paragraph adapted from the novel *The Crash* by Paul Kropp (2005), to create a series of sentences that all have the same subject–predicate format. Even though this is quite an exciting bit of text in the actual novel (see page 117), the modified version sounds slow and plodding because of the sluggish sentence structures. Have students work with a partner to choose two or three of the sentences to chunk and flip. (Students may want to compare their ideas to the actual text from the book, however this is not intended to be a matching game, but rather practice in crafting sentences.)

David Wisniewski's *The Secret Knowledge of Grown-ups* (2001) never fails to engage intermediate students with its silly hilarity. But it's also a great title for exemplifying different elements of craft.

A **preposition** is a word or phrase that indicates time (after, during) or location (in, near, beside) or some other relationship (about, instead of, like) between the subject and the other parts of a sentence.

If the prepositional phrase or subordinate clause is at the beginning of the sentence, it is usually separated from the rest of the sentence with a comma.

YOU DO: Have students read one of their pieces of writing to themselves and listen to the rhythm of the sentences. Think about whether any of the sentences should be flipped. Trust your ears and your head! If you want to emphasize one part of the sentence over another, the most important part should usually go first. Your ears will also let you know whether there should be a comma separating the two parts of the sentence.

If a group of sentences sounds plodding to the ear, take a closer look. Do they all have the same subject–predicate structure? Chunking and flipping just one or two sentences might be the solution to making the text sound more interesting and rhythmical.

ACTUAL TEXT FROM **THE CRASH:**

Up in front, Mrs. D was pumping the brake pedal like crazy....

I gripped the handrail as hard as I could while the bus slid and bumped across the road. Then there was the scream of metal crunching metal. We hit the metal guardail beside the road. If we were in a car, the rail would have bounced us back.

But we were in a school bus. We smashed over the guard rail, and the bus tipped sideways....

We were sliding down the hill....

The school bus would hit something—a bush or a rock—and the whole bus would shake. For a few seconds, it seemed like we were picking up speed. Then we smashed into something big. Wham! The whole bus flipped around, front to back.

And then it was quiet.

After the awful noise of crashing metal and bouncing down the hill, the silence was good. There was only the hiss of the bus now. For a few seconds, it had all stopped.

Flip the Sentence

Find at least two sentences to "flip."

Mrs. D was pumping the brake pedal like crazy up in front. I gripped the handrail as hard as I could as the bus slid and bumped across the snow. We hit a metal guardrail beside the road. The rail would have bounced us back if we were in a car. But we were in a school bus.

It seemed like we were picking up speed for a few seconds. We smashed into something big all of a sudden. Then it was quiet. The silence was good after the awful noise of crashing metal. There was only the hiss of the bus now. Everything stopped at last.

Pembroke Publishers © 2018 *Marvelous Minilessons for Teaching Intermediate Writing, Grades 3–8* by Lori Jamison Rog ISBN 978-1-55138-329-3

Chapter 8   Conventions: The Good Manners of Writing

> On the ester holliday's about five days after ester I got a black brand
> new cell phone and I was "exited" but all it needs is a charger to charge
> it. I would owas play with it like if it was oredy charged. Owe I can't wait
> to get a charger for it.

What's the first thing you notice about this piece of fourth-grade writing? The misspellings of *always* and *already*? The missing capital on *Easter* or the incorrect apostrophe on *holidays*? Or did you note that 45 of the 53 words in this passage are spelled correctly?

Unfortunately, errors in conventions tend to leap out at us in a manner that is disproportionate to their importance or quantity. And here's the thing about correct spelling and capitalization and punctuation and grammar: we do them as a courtesy for somebody else. If I'm the only one who's going to read my writing, it doesn't matter how I spell the words. It doesn't matter whether I ever use a capital or a period or smatter my writing with grammatical errors, as long as I can read it myself. But when I want someone else to read my writing, I owe it to them to use *conventional* grammar and spelling, and *conventional* punctuation and capitalization. That's why we call them "conventions." They are, quite simply, the good manners of writing.

Our challenge in intermediate grades is to set reasonable standards for correctness, while recognizing that they are still novices, still experimenting with the ways our language goes together. It's very difficult for our apprentice writers to balance correct conventions and elegant craft. That's why we have to teach both.

In primary grades, we encourage writers to use *invented* or *temporary* spelling to write words they don't know how to spell. Even in intermediate grades, we would prefer that the writer experiment with the spelling rather than avoid using a powerful word.

The reality is that most of our intermediate writers are still going to make the occasional error if they're taking risks with vocabulary. Although we are raising our expectations for correctness, we also know we have to pick our battles. For example, can we live with the nine-year-old writer in the example above spelling *excited* without the *c* and putting quotation marks around it for emphasis? Perhaps we should save our energy for ensuring that proper nouns have capitals and plurals don't have apostrophes? And the misspelling patterns of *always* and *already* provide us with important information about what to teach this student.

By the same token, our intermediate students should be able to write a simple sentence with correct grammar, punctuation, and capitalization. But as soon as they start experimenting with longer, more complex sentence structures, they are more likely to write run-on sentences or sentences with incorrect internal punctuation and mismatched verb tenses.

When it comes to fluent sentences, the line is somewhat blurred between conventions and craft. Conventions address the "correctness" of the sentence; craft focuses on the rhythm and flow. That's why you'll find several lessons related to sentence writing in the previous chapter. The lessons in this chapter address specific grammatical sentence structures: declarative (statement), interrogative (question), and exclamatory, as well as the imperative (command).

Writers put groups of words together in sentences and groups of sentences together in paragraphs. Expository writing tends to be easier to paragraph than narrative writing, because we start a new paragraph with each new subtopic (see Chapter 4, Writing to Inform). But it gets trickier in narrative writing, where paragraphing is arbitrary and often becomes a matter of style. (Think of James Joyce, author of *Ulysses*, who rarely used paragraphs at all.)

Paragraphing can vary considerably from one text to another. Newspaper articles, for example, have many short paragraphs, often comprising only one long sentence each. Novels are likely to have some long descriptive paragraphs full of many flowing sentences as well as very short paragraphs (or even one line) of dialogue. The only rule is that there is *no* rule about how many or what kinds of sentences belong in a paragraph.

I still believe that paragraphing is one of those developmental skills that students grow into as they become more sophisticated writers, but we need to nurture that growth. Expecting consistently correct paragraphing from fourth graders might be setting the bar too high, but that doesn't mean we can't introduce the concept and expect some effort at experimentation. I generally tell young writers: when in doubt, start a new paragraph. If it feels like there should be break in the narrative, it's probably a good time to start a new paragraph. In school and in tests, students are more likely to get credit for attempting a paragraph change than to get criticized for doing it incorrectly.

Grammar Rules We Thought We Knew (But Didn't)

Most of us were taught (and continue to teach our students) never to start a sentence with *and* or to end a sentence with a preposition. Well, it turns out that these aren't rules at all! In fact, Mark Forsyth, author of *The Elements of Eloquence*, calls the preposition rule "utter hogwash" and says that anyone who claims that you can't end a sentence with a preposition should be told *up to shut*. As for starting a sentence with "and", this belief has neither historical nor grammatical foundation. Grammarians assert that starting a sentence with a coordinating conjunction (the famous FANBOYS—for, and, nor, but, or, yet, so) still retains the grammatical integrity of the sentence. In fact, according to the Chicago Manual of Style, as many as 10 percent of the sentences in first-rate writing begin with conjunctions.

Actually, a *century of research* shows that traditional grammar instruction doesn't help—and might even hinder—student writing (Graham et al, 2012). But if we don't teach grammar, how will our students learn when to use quotation marks or whether to say *him and me* or *he and I*? We need to teach the conventions of our language in the context of actually using those conventions, ideally as minilessons during the Writing Workshop. And then we need to make our students accountable for applying and demonstrating what they've learned. Giving our students sentences to deconstruct or worksheets to complete at a separate time from expecting them to actually craft complete sentences of their own is a waste of everyone's time.

According to vocabulary expert Michael Graves, English consists of a very small number of frequent words, and an extremely large number of infrequent words.

- The 100 most frequent words account for almost 50% of the words in a typical text.
- The first 1,000 account for almost 70%.
- The first 5,000 account for almost 80%.
- The remaining 100,000 plus words account for the remaining 20%.

Is it Time to Stop Teaching Spelling?

In many languages, spelling isn't a subject in school. In fact, in Italian (and other languages), there's not even a word for spelling! What is it that makes English so much more difficult to read and write than many other languages?

Well, for one thing, most other languages aren't the hybrid that English is. We have many words filched directly from other languages (chauffeur, patio, kindergarten), and many more adapted from Latin and Greek (population, antique). In fact, over 60 percent of all English words have Greek or Latin roots (and when it comes to the sciences, the figure rises to over 90 percent of words.) And then there are acronyms like Radar *or* Scuba *and* portmanteau *words like* brunch *and* motel.

Here's another problem with English: there are so many words! The English language consists of about 200,000 words and only a handful of them can be considered "frequent." Over 100,000 words in English occur somewhere between one and nine times per 1,000,000 words in print. That means that when we teach an obscure (or even not so obscure) vocabulary word, chances are a student might need to read as many as 200 books before he encounters it again (Graves, 2009).

And let's face it, we haven't figured out a foolproof way to teach spelling. Essayists have been bemoaning the demise of spelling since the turn of the century (the 20th century, that is). Some people believe that spelling ability is innate; if you weren't born with it, you are consigned to a lifetime of relying on spellcheckers. And while it's true that spelling comes more easily to some people than others, there's no reason to give up. Everyone can learn some tools to make English spelling easier. Take a tip from the Italians—rather than teaching "spelling," build spelling instruction into overall "word study".

Word Study

A good word study program builds "word consciousness" through exposure to rich language, explicit teaching, and word play. According to vocabulary expert Michael Graves, there are two main elements to spelling as a part of word study: high frequency words and morphological patterns (i.e., prefixes, suffixes, and roots).

One hundred words make up 50% of English print. One thousand words account for 70%. No wonder they're called "high frequency"! We can live with our intermediate students misspelling *chaos* or *adjudicate*, but we simply can't accept *thay* or *becuz*. Not only are these words needed in pretty much everything our students write, most of them are not decodable. They just have to be internalized.

There are many lists of the 500 or 1000 most frequently-used words, easily accessible on the internet. Test your students on the first two hundred and then teach them as necessary, several per week. Then add the next two hundred, and so on. Mnemonics, raps, songs, actions—do whatever it takes for the students to be able to read and write these words automatically. Once taught, these are "no-excuse" words. They must be spelled correctly—every time.

Believe it or not, English is actually a language of patterns. The challenge is, the patterns of *meaning* often override the patterns of *sound*. When we study a family of related words such as *signature, signal,* and *designate,* we are better able to understand why *sign* has a silent *g*. As mentioned earlier, Greek and Latin are the foundation of the English language. This can be a fascinating study for students and teachers. You can find a list of the 30 most common Greek and Latin roots on page 133 (Yopp et al., 2008).

Many of the difficult words that our students encounter, however, are multi-syllabic, often with prefixes or suffixes or both. Smart spellers use words or parts of words that they know and combine them to form many other words.

While the other minilessons in this book focus on helping students get their writing "*good*," the lessons in this chapter focus on helping them get it "*right*." In this chapter you'll find a collection of lessons ranging from punctuation to spelling patterns to paragraphing to sentence types.

MINILESSONS IN THIS CHAPTER

Title	Page	Learning Focus
Be Your Own Editor	123	A self-editing routine for conventions
Sentence Stretching	124	Breaking narrative writing into paragraphs
Three Sentence Stories	126	Identifying and using different sentence types
The Royal Order of Adjectives	128	Sequence for using two or more adjectives
Possessive or Plural Word Sort	129	Using apostrophes in possessives but not plurals
Explode a Word	131	Identifying spelling patterns in groups with common roots
The Five Ps of Paragraphing	134	Building complex sentences

Be Your Own Editor

Editing for conventions is the last stage before publication in the publishing journey; it's what we do before sharing our writing with an audience. Our goal is for students to learn how to identify their own errors in conventions—and correct them. This editing routine asks writers to read each sentence twice, first for meaning and grammar, and a second time for spelling and conventions.

Learning Goal: Students will be able to find and correct their own errors in conventions before publishing a piece of writing.

I DO: Finding our own mistakes in spelling and punctuation might very well be the hardest part of the writing process. Remind students that when they first begin to write, they want to keep their ideas flowing. They spell and punctuate as well as they can, and don't worry too much about looking up words or making corrections. But before we share that writing with readers, we owe it to them to make our writing as correct as possible.

Display a short piece of writing with several errors in grammar, punctuation, spelling, and sentence structure. (This is not the best time to use a piece of your students' writing as an example; create your own or use an "anonymous" piece such as the sample at the beginning of this chapter.) Demonstrate for the students as you read it, sentence by sentence, thinking aloud about whether each one sounds like a complete sentence or whether the words sound grammatically correct. Then, get an "editing pen" (a brightly-colored skinny marker) and reread the piece, tapping each word as you read it. (Tapping each word with a marker leaves a dot under the word and helps students focus on individual words rather than overall meaning.) Circle any words that don't look correct. After reading the entire piece this way, go back to the circled words and use resources to find and correct the spellings.

> Unlike **revising**, which is all about making sure our ideas are clear and our words are powerful, **editing** is all about spelling and punctuating and capitalizing words correctly, so they can be read by someone else.

EDITING PROTOCOL

Read every sentence twice:

- First reading—Focus on sentences and grammar: Read each sentence aloud, listening to whether it "sounds right" grammatically. This is an opportunity to insert missing words, change words that sound grammatically incorrect, connect choppy sentences, or repair run-ons.
- Second reading—Focus on words and spelling: Use a skinny marker to "tap" each word, leaving a dot under it. If a word doesn't look right, circle it. At the end, go back to the circled words and use a dictionary or other resource to find the correct spellings.

WE DO: With another piece of writing, use an interactive writing approach with students sharing the pen as you collaboratively edit the piece for conventions.

YOU DO: Have students practice editing their own writing.

Sentence Stretching

Learning Goal: Students will be able to build complex sentences by expanding simple sentences.

I DO: We know that a complete sentence has to have a subject (who or what) and a predicate (is or does). That means "Joe ran" is a complete sentence. But writing would sound like a Grade One reader if all our sentences consisted of two or three words. We can make sentences more interesting by stretching them with a *when* or a *where* or a *why* or a *how*.

WE DO: Start with a basic sentence like "Students love writing." Write each word on an individual card and have three students stand at the front of the room, each holding a card. Use sticky notes to add capitals and periods. Now invite the students not standing to stretch the sentence by suggesting words, phrases, and clauses, such as:

- What kind of students? What kind of writing?
- When do they love writing?
- Where do they love writing?
- Why do they love writing?

As the students offer suggestions, write the words or phrases on cards and have the ones who made the suggestions come up and hold the cards. (My rule: Only the students still sitting can make suggestions; once you're standing, your job is just to smile and hold your card.) Guide the students to continue to build the complexity of the sentence.

If you feel your students need additional practice in sentence stretching, reproduce the graphic organizer on page 125.

YOU DO: Have students revisit a piece of their own writing to find a sentence that can be enhanced by adding a phrase or clause.

Stretch That Sentence!

When?	Where?	What Kind?	Who/What?	Is/Does	What?	Why?
			monkeys	climb		
			kids	play		
			scientists	study		
			teachers	say		

Three-Sentence Stories

There are actually only four different sentence types in English grammar and intermediate students should know how to use (and capitalize and punctuate) each one.

Learning Goal: Students will be able to identify and use all three (or four) sentence structures in a piece of writing.

I DO: Display the following excerpt from *My Brother Dan's Delicious* by Steven Layne where young Joey tries to convince an imaginary monster to eat his brother instead of him.

Point out that each of the sentences in the excerpt is a different type: a question, a statement, and an exclamation. If your students are unfamiliar with the three types of sentences, you might want to construct an anchor chart such as the one on page 127.

> Are there any monsters about? I just want you to know that my brother Dan's *delicious*. He's one ultratasty guy!

WE DO: Tell students that they're going to practice telling a story in just three sentences: a statement, a question, and a command. For example, I just won the lottery. I might say: *"Yippee, I won a million dollars! What will I do with all that money? I really should share it with my adorable students."* Invite students to help you construct a three-sentence story to tell that your bike just got stolen. Guide them to use a statement, a question, and an exclamation—in whatever order that makes the most sense.

You might want to give your students more opportunities for oral language practice before committing their ideas to paper. Have the students choose one of the prompts below to tell in three sentences.

> ### Three-Sentence Story Prompts
>
> — You're being punished for something you didn't do.
> — You just ate the worst food in the world.
> — You just saw the strangest thing.
> — You didn't get your homework done.
> — You were in the bathroom when the fire alarm went off.

YOU DO: The point of this exercise is not about telling a story in three sentences. It's about using different types of sentences to tell a story. Most of the sentences in our writing will be declarative, or statements. But the occasional question or exclamation can add interest and voice. (Asking a question is the easiest trick for adding voice to a piece of writing. This brings the reader into the text—the very definition of voice.)

Have students choose one of the drafts in their writing folder and use different coloured highlighters to highlight any exclamations or questions. Have them revise the piece by finding a place to add one (more) question and one (more) exclamation. They should read the piece out loud to themselves to ensure that the additions actually do flow smoothly.

Literature Link: Steven L. Layne's picture book *My Brother Dan's Delicious* contains examples of many types of sentence, punctuation, and grammatical constructions.

If your students are comfortable with the three main types of sentences, include the fourth: the command, or imperative.

Here's another example from Steven Layne's *My Brother Dan's Delicious*:

Do I hear the sounds of stomach growling coming from behind that basement door? Well, you just *stay put!* My brother Dan will be home soon. My brother Dan's delicious!

Types of Sentences

Sentence Type	Definition	Punctuation and Grammar	Example from *My Brother Dan's Delicious* by Steven Layne.
Statement (Declarative)	– the most common type of sentence – gives information or states a fact – does not require an answer or response from the reader	– period	*I just want you to know that my brother Dan's delicious.*
Question (Interrogative)	– asks a question – requires an answer from the reader	– question mark – generally starts with who, what, when, where, why, or how	*Are there any monsters about?*
Exclamation (Exclamatory)	– a sentence expressed with force or excitement	– exclamation mark	*He's one ultratasty guy!*
Command (Imperative)	– asks or tells someone to do something	– may have a period or exclamation mark, depending on forcefulness – the subject is not stated; it's understood to be you	*Well, you just stay put!*

The Royal Order of Adjectives

You can read more at
https://hip-books.com/
adjectives/

THE ROYAL ORDER OF ADJECTIVES

1. Article *(the)*, Number *(many)*, or Owner *(my)*
2. Opinion: What you feel about it (i.e. *beautiful, terrible*)
3. Physical Appearance: Size, Texture, Age, Shape, Color
4. Origin: Where it comes from
5. Material: What it is made of
6. Purpose: What it is for

Learning Goal: Students will be able to apply the correct grammatical order of two or more adjectives describing the same noun.

I DO: Remind students that adjectives are describing words that tell how big or what color or what size or what kind. One of the simplest rules of English is that an adjective always goes before the noun it describes. But that word order gets tricky when there's more than one adjective. Ask them to consider which sounds better: *big black dog* or *black big dog?* For those of us who speak English as our first language, we know the order of words by what sounds right. But there's actually a set of pretty strict rules about the order in which we write a series of adjectives.

WE DO: Suggest groups of two or three adjectives with a noun and have students work in pairs to determine what order they should go in. Some examples are provided in the box below. After practicing with a few examples, work together to construct a generalization about the order in which adjectives are listed. Supply students with a noun and three adjectives and have them determine the best order for the adjectives.

TABLE: plastic, modern, ugly
DINNER: buffet, delicious, huge
STORM: wind, dangerous, massive
SHIRT: heavy, woollen, red

Together, build an anchor chart of the correct order in which to list a string of adjectives, as in the example at the end of this lesson.

YOU DO: Have students revise their writing by looking for places where they might elaborate by inserting adjectives. Remind them, however, that it's more important to use the *right* word than a whole bunch of words! Only add modifiers if it makes the writing more clear and powerful.

Possessive or Plural Word Sort

That dastardly apostrophe! It just seems to insert itself in words whether it belongs or not. This word sort is intended to guide students in constructing their own generalizations about when to use an apostrophe. Word sorting is an excellent constructivist routine for helping students understand generalizations about our language.

Learning Goal: Students will be able to distinguish possessives and plurals, and use apostrophes appropriately.

I DO: Because this lesson routine takes a constructivist approach, there is not an explicit instruction component. However, you might want to refresh students' memories of what an apostrophe is.

You can find a word sort on possessives with and without apostrophes at: https://hip-books.com/teachers/writing-about-reading/that-dastardlyapostrophe/

WE DO: Reproduce the passage on page 130 and have students read it independently or read it aloud as they follow along. Point out that there are a number of words highlighted and underlined. After reading, they should work in pairs to sort those highlighted words into two columns: words with apostrophes and words without apostrophes. After sorting, the teams should work together to come up with a generalization about when to use apostrophes with the letter *s* and when not to use them. Discuss their generalizations and point out that we never use an apostrophe to make a word mean more than one (plural). Apostrophes are always used to show possession or ownership (other than in contractions, of course).

YOU DO: Send students into a piece of their own first draft writing with a highlighting pen and have them hunt for apostrophes, then ask themselves, "Is this a possessive or a plural?" and correct the punctuation, if necessary.

Possessive or Plural Word Sort

The <u>kids</u> were determined to drag their <u>parents</u> to the top of the mountain on the gondola. The <u>gondola's</u> car swung gently back and forth as it climbed. <u>Mom's</u> teeth chattered and <u>Dad's</u> face turned chalky white. But they were all <u>smiles</u> when they finally reached the mountaintop in the brilliant sun. The only thing that spoiled the <u>adults'</u> fun was dreading going back down again.

Sort the underlined words into two columns:

Words with apostrophes	Words without apostrophes

What do you notice about the difference between the words with apostrophes and the words without apostrophes?

Explode a Word

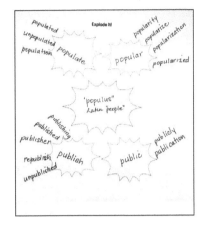

Learning Goal: Students will be able to generate a set of words from a common root, then identify spelling patterns.

I DO: Just like many branches can grow from a single tree root, many words can grow from a single root. Demonstrate for students how to explode words from a single root by adding prefixes and suffixes. Start with a word like *populi* (Latin for *people*) and show students how you can "explode it," by brainstorming as many words as possible related to that root.

WE DO: Invite students to add to the list in the example on the left. Talk about the connections of each of these words to the root word *populi*. Look at how endings change the part of speech and discuss the spelling changes that happen when you add endings.

YOU DO: Remind students to consider these spelling changes as they write other words with this root and these endings.

1. In the centre of the page, write the root and its meaning.
2. Around the word, record 4-6 words derived from that root.
3. Around each of those words, record as many forms of the word as possible, by adding prefixes and suffixes.

Explode It!

Pembroke Publishers© 2018 *Marvelous Minilessons for Teaching Intermediate Writing, Grades 3–8* by Lori Jamison Rog ISBN 978-1-55138-329-3

30 Most Common Greek and Latin Roots

Root	Meaning	Examples
-ast(er)-(G)	star	asteroid, astronomy, astronaut, asterisk
-audi- (L)	hear	audible, audience, auditory, auditorium
-auto- (G)	self	automatic, automate, autobiography, autograph
-bene- (L)	good	benefit, benign, benefactor, benevolent
-bio- (G)	life	biography, biology, biodegradable, symbiotic
-chrono- (G)	time	chronic, synchronize, chronicle, chronology
-dict- (L)	say	dictate, diction, edict, dictionary, addict
-duc- (L)	lead, make	deduce, produce, educator, conducive
-gen- (L)	give birth	gene, generate, generous, generation
-geo- (G)	earth	geography, geology, geometry, geopolitics
-graph- (G)	write	autograph, graphic, epigraph, demographic
-jur-, -jus- (L)	law	jury, justice, adjure, conjurer, justification
-log-, -logue- (L)	thought	logic, obloquy, apology, dialogue, analogy
-luc-, -lum- (L)	light	lucid, translucent, illuminate, elucidate
-man(u)- (L)	hand	manual, manure, manicure, manipulate
-mand-, -mend-	order	demand, recommend, remand, mandatory
-mis-, -mit- (L)	send	missile, transmission, emit, submit, permit
-omni- (L)	all	omnivorous, omnipotence, omniscient
-path- (G)	feel	empathy, pathetic, apathy, pathos, antipathy
-phil- (G)	love	philosophy, bibliophile, philanthropy
-phon- (G)	sound	phonics, telephone, euphony, microphone
-photo- (G)	light	photograph, photon, photocopy, photogenic
-port- (L)	carry	export, portable, rapport, deport, important
-qui(t)- (L)	quiet, rest	acquit, tranquil, requiem, quiescent
-scrib-, -script-	write	script, describe, transcribe, prescribe
-sens-, -sent- (L)	feel	resent, sensitive, sentence, sentient
-tele- (G)	far off	telecast, telephone, telekinesis, telepathy
-terr- (L)	earth	terrain, territory, extraterrestrial, terrace
-vac- (L)	empty	evacuate, vacate, vacancy, vacuous
-vid-, -vis- (L)	see	visible, video, envisage, invisible, revision

The Five Ps of Paragraphing

Knowing when to start a new paragraph in narrative writing is tricky, even for professional writers. Here are some guidelines to help writers "think in paragraphs."

Learning Goal: Students will be able to experiment with paragraphing a narrative text.

I DO: Paragraphs are tools for breaking up large blocks of text into manageable chunks for a reader. A change in paragraphs gives the reader some breathing space and signals that something is changing. In nonfiction, we start a new paragraph with each new topic or subtopic, but it's a little harder to decide when to start a new paragraph in narrative writing.

Although there are no hard and fast rules about when to start a new paragraph in a story, "the five Ps" offer some general guidelines (see the box in the margin). Display a passage such as the excerpt from *Shooting the Rapids* on page 135 to demonstrate the following reasons an author might start a new paragraph:

- **Person speaking:** Every time a new character speaks, we start a new paragraph, even if the previous character has only said one word.
- **Point in time:** Phrases like "later that night" or "the next day" are signals that the point in time is changing. When the time changes, so does the paragraph.
- **Place:** If the action moves from one location to another, it's a good time to change the paragraph.
- **Point of view:** If the narrative has been focusing on one character and shifts to another, change the paragraph.
- **Plot direction:** Often a change in the action signals a new paragraph.

WE DO: Invite the students to take a library book out of their desks and open it to any page. Encourage them to talk to a partner about whether the author of their books followed the "5 Ps" rule. For more practice, use the reproducible on page 136 for students to work in teams to edit into paragraphs. Have students work in pairs so they can discuss their paragraph choices.

YOU DO: Writers don't usually go back into a block of text to edit it for paragraphs; they tend to *think* in paragraphs. Often we allow students to write large blocks of text then go back in and edit it for paragraphs. Although this is a worthy exercise, in real-life writing, we want them to "think" in paragraphs, and as they're drafting, break the writing into chunks for themselves and their readers.

Here is how the author chose to paragraph this text excerpt from
***Shooting the Rapids* by Paul Kropp.**

We both paddled like crazy. In a minute, we had the canoe under control, but that minute cost us. We were at the start of the rapids.

"It's too late. We can't get to shore!" Timmy yelled. We were in the middle of the river, with rock ledges on both sides. Spray and foam shot up when the water hit a rock. The river sounded like thunder.

"Okay, we can do this!" I shouted to Timmy at the front of the canoe. "You tell me what's coming and I'll steer from the back."

The water pushed us forward like a speedboat. I had never gone so fast in a canoe before. Around us, water crashed into the rocks and shot into the air. It was almost like an amusement park ride. But this was no ride. It was real life. Boats crash in whitewater like this. We had only a chance of coming out alive.

THE FIVE Ps of PARAGRAPHING

Start a new paragraph when there is a change in:

- **P**erson speaking
- **P**oint in time
- **P**lace
- **P**erspective/ **P**oint of view
- **P**lot direction (action)

This is a good opportunity to teach the editing symbol for "start a new paragraph" (¶).

Paragraph Practice Activity

Place →	We pushed off from the shore. Some clouds had come up and it began to rain. *Great*, I said to myself. *All this, and now we're getting soaked.*
Plot direction change in action) →	Still, we kept going. We paddled until our hands were like raw meat. My shoulders ached. Even my butt and knees hurt. But we saw nothing on the shore, nothing ahead of us. The rain kept falling, and our hopes seemed to get washed away.
Point in time →	I think it was five o'clock when I heard my brother Timmy sniffling. He was up at the front of the canoe, so I couldn't see him.

"Timmy, are you okay?" I asked him.

Person speaking → "Yes …" he said at first. Then he turned back at me and I saw the hurt in his eyes. He'd been crying, but in the rain I couldn't see his tears. "No …" he said, and then he began wailing.

"Crying won't do any good," I said.

"But what … what are we going to do?" he wailed. "We've got no food. We're lost. Dad's sick …" and then the tears began again.

"It'll be okay," I told him.

"Connor, I'm scared," my brother cried.

Point of View → I said nothing more. The simple truth was too awful to say out loud. I was scared too.

Excerpt from *Shooting the Rapids* by Paul Kropp

Paragraph Practice

We both paddled like crazy. In a minute, we had the canoe under control, but that minute cost us. We were at the start of the rapids. "It's too late. We can't get to shore!" Timmy yelled. We were in the middle of the river, with rock ledges on both sides. Spray and foam shot up when the water hit a rock. The river sounded like thunder. "Okay, we can do this!" I shouted to Timmy at the front of the canoe. "You tell me what's coming and I'll steer from the back." The water pushed us forward like a speedboat. I had never gone so fast in a canoe before. Around us, water crashed into the rocks and shot into the air. It was almost like an amusement park ride. But this was no ride. It was real life. Boats crash in whitewater like this. We had only a chance of coming out alive.

from *Shooting the Rapids* by Paul Kropp

Resources

Bishop, A., Yopp, H. & Yopp, R. (2008). *Vocabulary Instruction for Academic Success.* Huntington Beach, CA: Shell Education.

Cunningham, P. (undated). *The Nifty Thrifty Fifty—50 Morphemic Key Words.* http://www.patcunninghamwfu. com/uploads/6/4/5/9/64599381/nifty_thrifty_fifty_words.pdf

Forsyth, M. (2013). *The Elements of Eloquence: How to Turn the Perfect English Phrase.* London: Icon Books.

Graham, S. & Perin, D. (2007). *Writing Next: Effective Strategies to Improve Writing of Adolescents in Middle and High Schools.* New York: Carnegie Corporation.

Graham, S. & Hebert, M.A. (2010). "Writing to read: Evidence for how writing can improve reading. A Carnegie Corporation Time to Act Report." Washington, DC: Alliance for Excellent Education.

Graham, S., McKeown, D., Kiuhara, S. & Harris, K. (2012). "A meta-analysis of writing instruction for students in the elementary grades." *Journal of Educational Psychology, 104,* 4.

Graves, M. (2016). *The Vocabulary Book: Learning and Instruction* (2nd Ed). New York: Teachers College Press.

Hattie, J. (2009). *Visible learning: A synthesis of over 800 meta-analyses relating to achievement.* London, New York: Routledge.

Hillocks, G. (1986). *Research on written composition: New directions for teaching.* Urbana, IL: ERIC Clearinghouse on Reading and Communication Skills & National Conference on Research in English.

Jacobson, J. (2010). *No More "I'm Done!"* Portland, ME: Stenhouse Publishers.

Juster, N. (1989). *As: A Surfeit of Similes.* New York: William Morrow & Co.

Kissner, E. (2006). *Summarizing, Paraphrasing and Retelling: Skills for Better Reading, Writing and Test Taking.* Portsmouth, NH: Heinemann.

Kohn, A. (1993). "Choices for Children: Why and How to Let Students Decide." *Phi Delta Kappan.* http://www.alfiekohn.org/article/choices-children/

Kropp, P. (2002). *Shooting the Rapids.* Toronto: High Interest Publishing.

——— (2002). *The Countess and Me.* Markham, ON: Fitzhenry & Whiteside.

——— (2005). *The Crash.* Toronto: High Interest Publishing.

——— (2003). *Ghost House.* Toronto: High Interest Publishing.

——— (2006). *Shooting the Rapids.* Toronto: High Interest Publishing.

——— (2007). *One Crazy Night.* Toronto: High Interest Publishing.

——— (2008). *Winner.* Toronto: High Interest Publishing.

Kropp, P & Rog, Lori Jamison (2004). *The Write Genre.* Markham, ON: Pembroke Publishers.

Marchisan, M. L. & Alber, S. R. (2001). "The write way: tips for teaching the writing process to resistant writers." *Intervention in School and Clinic, 36*(3), 154–162.

Marzano, R. J., Pickering, D. J. & Pollock, J. E. (2001). *Classroom instruction that works. Research-based strategies for increasing student achievement.* Alexandria, VA: Association for Supervision and Curriculum Development.

Mueller, P.A. & Oppenheimer, D. M. (2014). The pen is mightier than the keyboard: Advantages of longhand over laptop note-taking. *Psychological Science Online.*

National Governors Association Center for Best Practices, Council of Chief State School Officers (2010). *Common Core State Standards in Literacy.* Washington DC: National Governors Association Center for Best Practices.

Reeves, D. B. (2005). *Accountability in action: A blueprint for learning organizations (2nd Ed.)* Englewood CO: Advanced Learning.

Sidi, S. & Anderson, V. (2014). Situational interest and its impact on reading and writing. *The Role of Interest in Learning and Development, 13*(3).

Tompkins, G. (2000). *Teaching writing: Balancing process and product* (3rd Ed). Upper Saddle River, NJ: Merrill.

Tracy, K.N. (2013). "Writing to Read: Evidence for How Writing Can Improve Reading." *Literacy Daily.* https://www.literacyworldwide.org/blog/literacy-daily/2013/10/21/writing-to-read-evidence-for-how-writing-can-improve-reading

Wagner, T. (2008). "Rigor redefined. *Educational Leadership, 66*(2), 20–25.

Waterman, A., Havelka, J., Culmer, P., Hill, L. & Mon-Williams, M. (2017) *The ontogeny of visual–motor memory and its importance in handwriting and reading: a developing construct.* https://advancedenglishcurriculum.wordpress.com

Wiggins, G. & McTighe, J. (1998). *Understanding by Design* (2nd Ed). Alexandria, VA: Association for Supervision and Curriculum Development.

Yancy, K.B. (2009). *Writing in the 21st Century.* Urbana, IL: National Council of Teachers of English.

Index